Advance praise for

Transformative Leadership

"Transformation has been the goal of many leaders at least since Burns published his classic book *Leadership* in the 1970s. Carolyn M. Shields, however, asks an important follow-up question: Transformation for what? She critiques the answers found in the education field and distinguishes between the so-called transformational leadership discussed in that literature with an approach she dubs transformative leadership. Transformative leadership puts the promotion of social justice front and center in a leader's thoughts and actions. Shields' book, consequently, is more than an exercise in making linguistic distinctions; it provides unique answers to the what-do-I-do-Monday question for leaders intent on transforming schools and classrooms."

—*Robert Donmoyer, Professor, Leadership Studies, University of San Diego*

"This is a one-of-a-kind educational leadership book: part scholarly essay, part London Review of Books, part autobiographical experiences, and part leadership theory. Professor Carolyn M. Shields describes the ideas contained in *Transformative Leadership: A Primer* as both a way of life and a way of re-thinking. It weaves history into current events, illustrating each of the eight tenets of transformative leadership. The theory—originally presented in 2012—calls upon educators to responsibly engage in social change so as to create the pre-conditions for democratic teaching, learning, and leading. With this short text, a primer, Shields has established herself as the first Transformative Public Intellectual in the field of educational leadership. That, of course, is not a title she touts; rather, her humility and generosity as a scholar and teacher are evident on every single page as she credits many, many others for the wisdom she herself has attained and now is sharing with us. See if you agree. Here's one example of her challenging prose:

> Each time we remain silent, pushing an uncomfortable situation underground, we fail to help students grapple with difficult situations. And we fail to ensure that our schools are inclusive, enjoyable, and socially just places of learning. Moreover, we send the message that people experiencing these situations are somehow not 'normal.' We must learn to address uncomfortable situations, and in so doing, to make our schools more accepting and inclusive of diverse perspectives and backgrounds. (p.71)

—*Ira Bogotch, Professor of Educational Leadership, Florida Atlantic University*

Transformative Leadership

PRIMER

This book is part of the Peter Lang Education list.
Every volume is peer reviewed and meets
the highest quality standards for content and production.

PETER LANG
New York • Bern • Frankfurt • Berlin
Brussels • Vienna • Oxford • Warsaw

Carolyn M. Shields

Transformative Leadership
PRIMER

PETER LANG
New York • Bern • Frankfurt • Berlin
Brussels • Vienna • Oxford • Warsaw

Library of Congress Cataloging-in-Publication Data
Names: Shields, Carolyn M., author.
Title: Transformative leadership primer / Carolyn M. Shields.
Description: New York: Peter Lang, 2016.
Series: Peter Lang primers; v. 10
Includes bibliographical references and index.
Identifiers: LCCN 2015042704 | ISBN 978-1-4331-3197-4 (paperback: alk. paper)
ISBN 978-1-4539-1796-1 (e-book)
Subjects: LCSH: Leadership.
Classification: LCC HD57.7.S487 2016 | DDC 658.4/092—dc23
LC record available at http://lccn.loc.gov/2015042704

Bibliographic information published by **Die Deutsche Nationalbibliothek**.
Die Deutsche Nationalbibliothek lists this publication in the "Deutsche
Nationalbibliografie"; detailed bibliographic data are available
on the Internet at http://dnb.d-nb.de/.

The paper in this book meets the guidelines for permanence and durability
of the Committee on Production Guidelines for Book Longevity
of the Council of Library Resources.

© 2016 Peter Lang Publishing, Inc., New York
29 Broadway, 18th floor, New York, NY 10006
www.peterlang.com

Printed in the United States of America

Contents

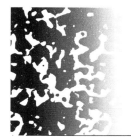

Understanding Leadership Theories

I hope to demonstrate that the processes of leadership must be seen as part of the dynamics of conflict and of power; that leadership is nothing if not linked to collective purpose; that the effectiveness of leaders must be judged not by their press clippings but by actual social change.

—Burns, 1978, p. 3

There are competing theories and competing practices, and it is our role as administrators, individuals of action, to sort among them ... A critical theory is necessary; to encourage us to view events in historical perspective, to doubt the validity of received truth (...), and to continue our search for more adequate solutions to our problems.

—Foster, 1986, p. 13

Why Do We Need Yet Another Leadership Theory?

Leadership is purposeful, moral, collective action that leads to social change. It is diffuse and does not reside solely in any one individual but recognizes the power of collective action.

My response to the question of why another primer on educational leadership lies in the quotations with which this chapter opens. Pulitzer Prize–winning scholar James McGregor Burns, in his seminal work simply called *Leadership* (1978), argued that the impact of leadership should be judged by *actual social change*. Approximately a decade later, educational leadership scholar William Foster asserted the need for a critical theory of leadership to judge from among the myriad theories to discover "*more adequate solutions* to our problems." And there definitely is a myriad of theories.

In the 2010 *International Encyclopedia of Education*, there are 47 chapters relating to different aspects of educational leadership. Moreover, the 2002 *Second International Handbook of Educational Leadership and Administration* (Leithwood & Chapman) comprised 34 chapters, and indeed, the list of handbooks, edited books, authored books, and chapters related to educational leadership is virtually endless. However, the quest for an appropriate theory of leadership is not new. We have looked to historical giants of the past, including the military commanders Sun Tzu and Alexander the Great; politicians such as Machiavelli, Lincoln, and Churchill; entrepreneurs like Steve Jobs; athletes and coaches like Vince Lombardi and John Wooden; and other diverse individuals including Warren Buffet, Pope Francis, and even Jesus Christ. Leadership has been broken down into seven habits (Covey, 1989), 21 irrefutable laws (Maxwell & Ziglar, 2007), five levels (Maxwell, 2013), nine steps (Martens, 2015), seven simple secrets (Stone, 2014), and so on. In fact, at the time of writing Amazon.com lists 138,733 books on leadership. In education alone, Amazon.com lists 29,409 books, to say nothing of the countless chapters and articles indexed in scholarly and not so scholarly publications.

The argument of this primer and the underlying impetus for *transformative leadership* is that,

even taken together, many popular, current theories have not resulted, and will not result, in either "actual social change" or "more adequate solutions to our problems"—including problems associated with social exclusion, the education "empowerment" or "achievement gap," and the preparation of democratic citizens. Hence, I will argue here that a new, critical, and radically different approach to leadership is necessary. Although leadership is a pressing issue in many fields, including non-profit, social services, or governmental agencies such as police and firefighting, my focus in this primer will be on *educational* leadership. At the same time, I firmly believe that transformative leadership is a way of thinking and living that can guide leadership in numerous other fields as well.

Neither transformative leadership nor social justice is an add-on, something to fit into the school leader's busy day. It is an essential underpinning of significant transformation. And transformation is the necessary pre-condition for creating learning conditions under which all children, regardless of social situation, identity markers, or home background, will be able to succeed.

In this chapter, I will first briefly examine the current socio-political context for public education, some factors exacerbating the ability of educational organizations to support the creation of a strong and deeply democratic society, and the inadequacy of many popular leadership theories to respond to the need. The chapter will conclude with an overview of *transformative* leadership in which I introduce its potential for deep and significant change.

The 21st Century Context

I recall once making a conference presentation with a young doctoral student who began our paper with the following quote by Maxine Greene (1998):

Social justice education means teaching to the end of arousing a consciousness of membership, active and participant membership in a society of unfulfilled promises—teaching for what Paulo Freire used to call "conscientization" (1970), heightened social consciousness, a wide-awakeness that might make injustice unendurable. (p. xxx)

To our surprise, she was immediately interrupted by someone from the back of the room asking, "What do you mean by unfulfilled promises?" We were astounded at the time, and I continue to be surprised when my students fall silent in response to this question. Our society (and many others) founded on what we like to think of as democratic principles, purports to offer to every individual certain liberties and protections without regard to race, gender, religious practice, and so on. Nevertheless, one would likely have to have lived in an isolation tank not to be aware of the many social, economic, and cultural challenges of the 21st century.

The problems that need solutions—both social and educational—have not abated. As I write, the media is consumed with violence—shootings and other violence in schools, the killings of young Black males in numerous cities around the United States, gang violence, inappropriate police actions, and so forth. The financial state of the nation's largest cities is precarious as many cities teeter on the edge of bankruptcy or, like Detroit (where I live), have emerged from under the governance of emergency management, still to be confronted by a plethora of serious challenges. Corporations decry trade agreements that may result in the loss of jobs to underemployed countries while salaries of corporate executives continue to increase exponentially. In fact Piketty, of the Paris School of Economics, found that the proportion of income accumulated by the top 10% of earners in the United States has grown from 33.5% in 1960 to 47.9% in 2010; moreover, these higher wages

accounted for two-thirds of the increase in American income inequality over the last four decades (Eavis, 2014). The income gap continues to widen in almost every developed country, with a 2015 Oxfam report announcing that by 2016 the richest 1% of the world's population will own more than all the rest, having "seen their share of global wealth increase from 44 percent in 2009 to 48 percent in 2014 and at this rate will be more than 50 percent in 2016" (Byanyima, 2015).

New security threats, including natural disasters, global warming, terrorism, identity theft, and many others, continue to preoccupy scholars and politicians alike. Globally, poverty affects nearly half of the world's population, with more than 3 billion people living on less than $2.50 a day, 850 million of them experiencing hunger daily, and 750 million lacking access to clean drinking water.[1] Poverty is also rampant in the United States despite President Lyndon Johnson's 1964 emotional appeal for war on poverty—a war, he said, we cannot afford to lose. In fact, approximately 12 million American children live under the poverty line, and 1.6 million of them experience homelessness in a given year. Moreover, "Black and Hispanic children were more than twice as likely to live in poverty in 2007 as non-Hispanic white and Asian children" (Moore, Redd, Burkhauser, Mbwana, & Collins, 2009).

The unemployment rate is twice as high for non-Whites as for Whites, with a strong negative correlation between levels of schooling completed and unemployment (NCES, 2010, p. vi). In certain metropolitan regions the unemployment rates for all are unacceptable, with Detroit topping the list at 24.8% of the population unemployed (BLS, 2015). There, unemployment is compounded by many factors, not the least of which is the

---

1   These statistics come from multiple United Nations agencies including World Health, UNICEF, and the Food and Agriculture Organization.

47% rate of adult illiteracy (Nearly Half of Detroit's Adults, 2011). Other challenges relate to our "justice" system in which, although the United States comprises 5% of the world population, it has 25% of the world's prisoners. "Together, African American and Hispanics comprised 58% of all prisoners in 2008, even though African Americans and Hispanics made up approximately one quarter of the US population" (NAACP, 2015). The NAACP report continues, "Nationwide, African-Americans represent 26% of juvenile arrests, 44% of youth who are detained, 46% of the youth who are judicially waived to criminal court, and 58% of the youth admitted to state prisons" (Center on Juvenile and Criminal Justice). Sometimes known as the school-to-prison pipeline, the impact of school failure or suspensions is particularly salient here.

Evidence of inequity in our society could consume more pages than available in this volume; however, the injustice is apparent. Civil society seems to be in disarray, and many would argue that part of the reason is the failure of public schools to promote democratic citizenship. Barber, for example, asserts:

> For true democracy to flourish ... there must be citizens. Citizens are men and women educated for excellence—by which I mean the knowledge and competence to govern in common their own lives. The democratic faith is rooted in the belief that all humans are capable of such excellence and have not just the right but the capacity to become better citizens. (2001, pp. 12–13)

Here, the phrase "in common" is of particular importance as it suggests the kind of agreement and mutuality advocated by Judith Green (1999) in her conception of "deep democracy." Giroux reiterates the argument, suggesting,

> On the national level, it is rare to hear legislators, educators, or parents talk about schools in ways

Deep democracy is a robust form of democracy that focuses both on processes such as voting and on content such as mutual benefit and equity.

that suggest that they embody society's commitment to a democratic future and offer students a
space in which they can be honored, critically engaged, and nurtured with a sense of dignity and
hope. (2009, p. 9)

In fact, he suggests that democracy may be
"fatally wounded, as those who are young, poor,
immigrants, or people of color are excluded from
the operations of power, the realm of politics, and
crucial social provisions" (p. 9).

The point here is that until we transform our
education system into one that is more equitable,
inclusive, and socially just; until all students from
whatever backgrounds have equal opportunities to
participate, thrive, and succeed, national social
and economic unrest will continue to challenge
the well-being of democratic society both in the
United States and throughout the world.

The Educational Context

Yet, even as civil society is increasingly cracked
and fragmented, education, seen by many as the
solution to society's challenges, appears equally
challenged and endangered. Many school districts—
especially in major urban areas—are vulnerable
to closure, bankruptcy, or, at minimum, declining
enrollment, slashed budgets, and renewed threats
of school takeovers either by for-profit corporations
or legislatures themselves. Even as the wealth gap
between the top and bottom segments of the population affects the well-being of individuals, discrep-
ancies in school funding also threaten the very
existence of schools in many communities.

Although in 2011–2012, U.S. public high schools
recorded an all-time high four-year graduation rate
of 80%, graduation rates continue to vary greatly
by state and race. "Nationwide, Black students
graduated at a rate of 69 percent; Hispanics graduated at 73 percent; Whites graduated at a rate of 86

percent" ("State High School Graduation Rates," 2015). Moreover, these rates belie further inequities in educational opportunity.

The need for deep and equitable change in education is almost irrefutable and, as the 2014 USDE study found, begins in pre-school and permeates every aspect of American education. These researchers found well-known disparities related to retention and high school graduation, but also reported lesser-known data about access to higher-level courses in high school, and suspension and discipline rates in pre-school. Disproportionate representation of African American students in disciplinary incidents, suspension, and special education classes has long been known; for example, "35% of black children grades 7–12 have been suspended or expelled at some point in their school careers compared to 20% of Hispanics and 15% of whites" (NAACP, 2015). In their study, the authors actually found disproportionate rates of suspension begin in kindergarten, where "Black students represent [only] 18% of preschool enrolment but 42% of students suspended once, and 48% of the students suspended more than once." (Other studies, as we shall see later, found that suspensions actually begin in pre-school.) They further found that schools serving large percentages of poor and minoritized[2] students often have fewer resources, fewer advanced-level courses, and lower graduation rates. Specifically, they found that "less than half of American Indian and Native-Alaskan high school students have access to the full range of math and science courses in their high school" and that the graduation rate in 2005 in urban areas, where there are higher concentrations

---

2 I use the term *minoritized* here (as I have done elsewhere) instead of the more common word *minority* to suggest that regardless of whether some groups are in the numerical minority or not, they may still experience minority status due to an imbalance of power relations.

of poor and minoritized students, was 53% "compared with 71 percent in the suburbs."

LGBTQ refers to people who are lesbian, gay, bisexual, transgendered, or "queer"—a term adopted by LGBT people themselves to diffuse its negative meaning; however, the Q is also often used to mean "questioning."

Similarly, LGBTQ children experience verbal harassment, physical harassment, and physical assault at school and more than 50% reported that they heard their teachers or other school staff making homophobic remarks (Kosciw, Greytak, Palmer, & Boesen, 2014). According to some sources, roughly 40% of unaccompanied homeless youth are LGBTQ, compounding their challenges in terms of day-to-day living and, certainly, in getting a good education.

At a time when there are few countries in which income inequality is rising faster than in the United States, compelling data demonstrate clear correlations between education and poverty as well as poverty and race. Coley and Baker (2013) found, for example, that

> More than one in five U.S. children live in "official" poverty today, with an even higher rate for Black and Hispanic children and for those in families headed by a single parent. Among the world's 35 richest countries, the United States holds the distinction of ranking second highest in child poverty [and] the achievement gap between the poor and the non-poor is twice as large as the achievement gap between Black and White students. (p. 3)

Poverty, often associated with high levels of crime in low-income neighborhoods, increased health problems, sparseness of books in homes, and malnutrition, is strongly correlated with poor educational outcomes. And, to make matters worse,

> less than one-quarter of homeless elementary school students nationwide are proficient in math (21.5%) and reading (24.4%), as opposed to over one-third (39.6% and 33.8%, respectively) of their housed peers. Homeless high school students are even less likely to be proficient in these subject

areas (11.4% in math and 14.6% in reading, versus 32.2% and 30.9%, respectively). (ICPH, 2013)

The situation is equally disparate—and desperate—for children who are minoritized because of ethnicity, home language, religious persuasion, sexual orientation, or other factors beyond their control.

The statistics are endless, but the reality is that there are real children beneath the numbers. We must acknowledge that no child chooses to be poor or homeless or gay. No child wants to be hungry, to have to worry about the survival of his or her family, or where they will find shelter for the night. No child wants to attend school without clean clothes or adequate school supplies. Few would choose to be different from their peers in any way. Yet, these and many other factors beyond their control affect the ability of many children to succeed in school and, conversely, the ability of schools to educate them.

This situation is, however, not hopeless. We cannot continue to simply point to the lived realities of large proportions of our society, throw up our hands, and say that until or unless these societal disparities are remedied, educational outcomes will continue to be unequal. It may be more difficult to educate children who come from challenging home circumstances, but it is our job. Educators are too well aware of the notion that we can predict school success by parents' levels of education and employment. Yet, in developed countries if we allow this situation to continue, we are abrogating the very responsibility for which we have signed on. Public education must be for all—the most vulnerable as well as the most advantaged.

A Renewed Call for Leadership

Numerous scholars have asserted the importance of educational leadership in assuring the achievement

of all students—and hence, in redressing inequities. In fact, there are many who argue that without strong and excellent leadership, school reform is unlikely to succeed (Dimmock & Goh, 2011; Marks & Printy, 2003). Further, researchers have found that leadership has "profound implications for student and school outcomes" (Leithwood & Jantzi, 1999; Miller, Brown, & Hopson, 2011). At the same time, may others decry the failure of educational leaders to "engage in transformative leadership practices with an emphasis on leading for social justice" (Boske, 2012, p. 184). Anello, Hernandez, and Khadem (2014) begin their discussion of transformative leadership with the statement, "The world is calling for a new model of leadership that effectively addresses today's challenges"; they state, "Formulas, gimmicks and easy answers have proven their bankruptcy" (p. 1). I believe that it would be accurate to add that the numerous leadership theories and reform efforts of the last century have failed to provide high quality education for everyone. Moreover, I believe that this has much to do with the ways in which leadership has been conceptualized and with the inadequacies of many of the current, dominant leadership theories.

First, it is important to note that I am framing the urgency as a need for new forms of leadership—not simply for new leaders who occupy formal roles within an organization. As Ogawa and Bossert claimed in 1995, leadership should not be considered "the province of a few people in certain parts of organizations [but rather] as a quality of organizations—a systemic characteristic" (p. 225). Their argument is that leadership does not rely solely on the individual characteristics and attributes of those in formal roles, or in their behaviors, but that it depends on relationships and interactions. Leadership, they posit, "flows through the networks of roles that comprise organizations" (p. 238). Leadership flows up and down and within levels as teachers are influenced by parents and students, as board members

are influenced by principals and teachers, as principals are influenced by caretakers and by local business owners, and so on. The perspectives of all—their abilities, needs, and wants—influence the ways in which the organization develops. Hence, leadership is a broad and fluid concept that flows through "networks of roles" (p. 225).

Second, in 2006, Oakes and Rogers argued the need for a radically different approach to school reform, asserting, "Technical changes themselves, even in the hands of committed and skillful professional "change agents" or backed by court orders, are too weak to interrupt the intergenerational transmission of racial inequality." They then claim that those who seek reform have "not treated equity reforms as distinctly different from other school improvement initiatives" (pp. 21–22), but have relied on strategies to "increase educators' capacity and to make school structures and organizational cultures more hospitable to effective practices" (p. 22). The focus, unfortunately, is consistent with many of the scientific approaches to leadership that arose in business and industry in the early 20th century, one that emphasizes technical and managerial aspects, with little attention being paid to context or to the political nature of education. Oakes and Rogers state:

> As in the business world, these change strategies make sense as long as all parties to the reform share a common goal. But efforts to address race and class inequality uncover conflicting interests. ... Quite simply, educational equity is entangled with cultural and political dynamics that extend beyond the school; therefore, equity reforms must engage issues of power by extending beyond the school. (p. 31)

Further, they assert that in most reform strategies, "Because of a political dynamic in which the existence, let alone the distribution, of power is never explicitly addressed, technical change strategies tend toward consensus rather than conflict" (p. 32). The problem is that when ideology comes into play, consensus is rarely possible.

In the next section, as I provide a brief description of some of the most popular leadership theories, the ostensible neutrality of the theories, their focus on individual leaders, and their failure to address social, cultural, political, or economic dynamics, or to call for radical reconstruction of the norms of schooling will become apparent. A critical approach to transforming leadership that both acknowledges these factors and calls for action to redress them is long overdue.

Recent Approaches to Leadership

In 1998, Leithwood and Duke conducted a review of leadership theories dating from 1988 and identified those most frequently mentioned or studied. They found that

> twenty specific leadership concepts were explicitly mentioned in the 121 articles. Most frequently mentioned specific concepts of leadership were instructional leadership (16 mentions), leadership styles (12), and transformational leadership (11). (p. 32)

Although this ignores the 82 other less frequently mentioned theories, for the purposes of this chapter, I will briefly focus on these three concepts: instructional leadership, transformational leadership, and several additional theories that fall under the broad category of leadership styles, including theories of moral or ethical leadership, participative or distributed leadership, and democratic leadership. Although the lines among these theories blur, they are distinct enough to demonstrate their foci, their strengths, as well as those elements that appear to be neglected.

Instructional Leadership

Instructional leadership has been found to be among the most studied forms of leadership in the last quarter century. Leithwood and Duke explain that instructional leadership "typically assumes that the critical focus for attention by leaders is the behaviors of teachers as they engage in activities directly affecting the growth of students" (p. 34). Hallinger, Leithwood, and Heck (2010) assert, "Principal instructional leadership grew out of research on instructionally effective schools conducted during the mid-to-late 1970s" (p. 18). The model, as shown in figure 1.1 below, includes three major tasks—defining the school mission, managing the instructional program, and creating a positive school climate—each containing several sub-categories of activities. The authors conclude, "The preponderance of evidence indicates that school principals contribute to school effectiveness and student achievement indirectly through actions they take to influence school and classroom conditions" (p. 21).

There can be no doubt that attending to the instructional program of the school is a key role for school leaders. Unless all students are included in an engaging, high quality learning environment designed for each to develop the skills, knowledge, and dispositions necessary for both personal success and civic citizenship, the school is not fulfilling its responsibility as a public institution. Yet, an examination of the model presented by Hallinger and Murphy in 1985 shows no attention to disparities, sub-groups, or disaggregated data. Instead, the clear focus is the organization as a whole. Monitoring student progress, protecting instructional time, and the like are certainly necessary activities for school leaders; however, it is important to note that there have been numerous critiques of the school improvement movement, identified as the source of instructional leadership models. For example, Trujillo and Renée (2013) state that using standardized tests as the measure of

effectiveness "led to narrow conceptions of student success and the purposes of education—ignoring the social, civic, and broader academic aspects of schooling" (p. 20). This focus, they argue, emphasizes the economic function of education to the exclusion of other important factors.

Figure 1.1. Instructional management framework. From Hallinger and Murphy (1985).

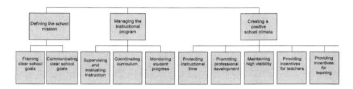

Their final critique is important:

> Finally, these research traditions were critiqued for their inadequate treatment of the socio-political and normative contexts of schooling (Weiner 2003; Oakes & Lipton 2003; Thrupp & Willmott 2003; Oakes & Rogers 2006). The studies discounted the inherently political nature of schools, as seen in issues of who has access to power and resources, who can make decisions, and how resources are allocated. (pp. 2–21)

The focus on behaviors (rather than underlying beliefs, values, and assumptions), the lack of attention to issues of power, combined with a lack of attention to socio-political and normative contexts of schooling are major differences between instructional leadership and *transformative* leadership as will be explicated below.

Transformational Leadership

The second major approach to leadership identified in Leithwood and Duke's study, and one that has been extremely influential in the subsequent years, is transformational leadership. In fact, the authors acknowledge that there have been several

conceptions of transformational leadership (including those by Burns, 1978; Kowalski & Oates, 1993; and Bennis & Nanus, 1985), but they assert, "The most fully developed model of transformational leadership in schools has been provided by Leithwood and his colleagues" (p. 35). Originally conceptualized with eight dimensions each with sub-categories, the more recent iterations by Leithwood comprise four major dimensions: setting directions, developing people, redesigning the organization, and managing the instructional program. Within each of these categories are additional activities as outlined in figure 1.2 below.

In his 2010 article, Leithwood addresses one critique of transformational leadership—that it overlapped with other views of leadership—by saying,

> If, as in this case, the goal is to develop a model of leadership that incorporates practices which reflect the best evidence about what works, then lack of distinguishing features is inevitable and certainly not a weakness. (p. 162)

He addressed a possible critique that the model draws on personality traits by emphasizing that the "school-specific model … includes only behaviors or practices that almost anyone with an interest in leadership could learn" (p. 162). Here again, I offer a critique similar to that advanced by Trujillo and Renée (2013) that the socio-political and normative contexts of schooling are ignored, as are the underlying beliefs, values, and assumptions that are so important in shaping practice. Blackmore (2011) reminds us that transformational leadership, in addition to instructional leadership, has been "framed narrowly" from within the school improvement–school effectiveness traditions, and hence, "appropriates critical perspectives while depoliticising their social justice intent" (p. 21). Moreover, these theories fail to address the three criteria advanced by Foster (1983) for an adequate theory of educational administration: that it be "explanatory, social, and critical" (p. 3).

Figure 1.2. Transformational Leadership based on Leithwood (2010).

Transformational Leadership	
Setting Directions	Building a shared vision
	Fostering the acceptance of group goals
	High-performance expectations
Developing people	Providing individualized support/consideration
	Intellectual stimulation
	Providing an appropriate model
Redesigning the organization	Building collaborative cultures
	Restructuring
	Building productive relationships with families and communities
	Connecting the school to its wider environment
Managing the instructional program	Staffing the program
	Providing instructional support
	Monitoring school activity
	Buffering staff from distractions to their work

Leadership Styles

Early literature related to leadership traits found little evidence that individual characteristics could be consistently associated with "good" leadership. Factors such as age, years of experience, formal educational training, charisma, and so forth are inconclusive, even irrelevant, for it has long been acknowledged that there are many different types of "good" (excellent and ethical) leaders. Thus, in 1998, Leithwood and Duke changed the language and referred to leadership styles instead of traits. Among the styles they identified were moral, participative, managerial, and contingent leadership. Managerial leadership, often identified with the classical management literature that focuses on the technical aspects of leadership, including the functions, tasks, and roles necessary for the efficient

operation of the organization, and with transactional leadership, is both well entrenched and well known. Although technical activities are necessary, much has been written about the negative impact of emphasizing the rational, technical, or scientific aspects to the exclusion of other aspects of an organization.

Contingent Leadership. This approach, also known as situational leadership (Blake & Mouton, 1964; Hersey & Blanchard, 1977), emphasizes that different situations and contexts require different forms of leadership. It "assumes that what is important is how leaders respond to the unique organizational circumstances or problems which they face as a consequence of, for example, the nature and preferences of coworkers, conditions of work, and tasks to be undertaken" (Leithwood & Duke, p. 39). To assess the dominant form of leadership behavior, Hersey and Blanchard identified what they thought of as two opposing approaches—task-oriented and relations-oriented behaviors. Once again, what is important here is not the four dimensions of leadership that arise from a quadrant analysis of these styles, but the recognition of the importance of context to the leadership role—a recognition that continues to be important today. Thus, Leithwood's notion that there is considerable overlap among theories when one is seeking to determine some of the best practices for leaders is important, for elements of many of these theories are apparent in most recent leadership theories.

Moral Leadership. Moral leadership acknowledges, "Values are a central part of all leadership and administrative practice" (Leithwood & Duke, p. 35). This is important because, whether the underlying values are explicit or implicit, they drive much of what occurs within an organization. More recent iterations of this concept include what is often called *ethical leadership* (Ciulla, 2005; Furman, 2004; Langlois, 2011; Starratt, 1991) or *authentic leadership* (Terry, 1993). The common thread in all of these approaches to leadership is that of a guiding

moral purpose that directs leadership actions and organizational goals. The difficulty, of course, is who determines the values to be adopted, and what happens when there are competing value positions within the organization. Nevertheless, a strong sense of moral purpose permeates most current leadership theories and is certainly inherent in the concept of *transformative* leadership.

Participative Leadership. Notions of participative leadership are to be found in early organizational theories, for example in the work of Mary Parker Follett (1940/1973), who posited the need for "a relation between leaders and led which will give to each the opportunity to make creative contributions to the situation" (p. 255). In 1979, Schwartz and Ogilvy posited the need for what they termed *heterarchic leadership* in recognition that no one person has all of the requisite skills to lead an organization and, hence, that the role must rotate depending on the situation. More recently, the term is attributed to Yukl (1994), who describes leadership that encompasses shared contributions by members of a group. Distributed or distributive leadership can also fall into this category, recognizing again the complexity of leadership in a VUCA (volatile, uncertain, complex, and ambiguous) world.[3] Most leadership theories, including that of *transformative leadership* to be advanced here, include recognition that leadership is shared, as Ogawa and Bossert indicate, a quality of the organization, and not a heroic and solitary activity.

Democratic Leadership. Although Leithwood and Duke do not list democratic leadership as a distinct category, they indicate that it could fall within either moral or participative categories. I identify it here as a separate category because of its importance and long history in Western thought. Moreover, democratic leadership not only overlaps

---

3   VUCA, a concept I have written about elsewhere (Shields, 2013), originated in the military in recognition that the contexts in which we live and work are volatile, uncertain, complex, and ambiguous.

with the previously mentioned approaches, but with the more recent emphasis on leadership for social justice. Möller (2010), for example, describes democratic leadership as "a moral activity which cannot be fully grasped without including a discussion of what we mean by an education based on democratic values" (p. 12). She goes on to posit that democratic leadership implies:

> The primary responsibility of education is to create democratic citizens, a conviction that a more democratic and egalitarian organization of society is both possible and desirable, and that education can have an important role to play in attaining this kind of society. (p. 12)

Even though the balance has shifted away from democratic ideals, the concept has long been part of organizational studies, with Mary Parker Follett writing a century ago, "Democracy is an infinitely including spirit ... We have an instinct for democracy because we have an instinct for wholeness; we get wholeness only through reciprocal relations, through infinitely expanding reciprocal relations" (1918, p. 157). In education, discussion of democratic leadership often harkens back to Dewey's notions of democracy as both a form of government and a way of living together. Möller explains Dewey's perspective: "The development of truly democratic communities is restricted by our inability to critically examine currently held assumptions, and these habits are learned in schools" (p. 12). The notion of critique is particularly important, given the position that leadership must be both critical and educative if it is to be successful in transforming education (Blackmore, 2011; Foster, 1982, 1983; Shields, 2011). At the same time, as important as is the concept of democratic leadership, as a theory it is relatively ill-defined and offers little guidance for leaders wanting to reform or restructure their organizations.

Taken together these theories, and many others, including servant (Greenleaf & Spears, 1998), bridge (Tooms & Boske, 2010), and leadership for social

justice (Brooks & Tooms, 2008; Theoharis, 2007) include aspects of leadership that meet the criteria of the two initial quotations: critical leadership that includes an examination of the dynamics of power and conflict that focuses on real social change, and that offers more adequate solutions to deep-seated social problems. For that reason, although *transformative leadership* is a distinctly different theory, grounded in critical perspectives, and positing explicit values of inclusion, equity, and social justice, aspects of many other theories may be found within its tenets. Caldwell, Dixon, Floyd, Chaudoin, Post, and Cheokas (2012) explain: "Transformative leadership integrates ethical mandates, behavioral assumptions, and standards of excellence which are fundamental requirements for the effective governance of organizations" (p. 176).

One final note of caution must be sounded. Leadership theories, for the most part, are intended to offer guidance and some underlying principles to help leaders ground their practices. Few are comprehensive. In general they do not offer a how-to guide or recipe for dealing with the myriad of situations one encounters, but comprise a lens through which to view one's daily work.

Wrigley (2013) offers an acerbic critique of the foregoing models, arguing,

> The officially promoted models of school evaluation and change ... hinder a genuine rethinking of educational institutions and activity, and serve at a meta level to obstruct meaningful change in pedagogy, curriculum, structures and relationships. They operate within a policy environment where, paradoxically, an insistence on modernisation and improvement disguises the lack of transformative rethinking, and the mantra of "mission, vision and values" serves as aesthetic and spuriously ethical camouflage for the reorientation of education to primarily economic functions (Ball, 2008). With honourable exceptions, the frantic productivity of effectiveness and improvement experts is marked

by the absence of a critical debate about educational purpose. (p. 31)

His critique, although perhaps sharper than many, is consistent with the comments made by Blackmore (2011) above, with the call of Oakes and Rogers for equity-oriented leadership, and with my own conviction that *transformative* learning and leadership offer a way forward.

Transformative Leadership

Transformative leadership is a critical theory of leadership that challenges organizational structures as well as dominant beliefs, values, and assumptions, and leads to more equitable and inclusive educational opportunities and deeply democratic societal outcomes for all.

Transformative leadership is as much a way of life and a way of (re)thinking as it is a leadership theory. It does not address the specifics of budgeting or personnel management or facility construction or many other tasks a school leader may encounter; however, it does offer a set of underlying tenets that can guide these and all other decisions leaders will be called upon to make. In other words, it is a lens through which to carefully examine all aspects of schooling.

Although most theories of transformational leadership reference Burns's (1978) work as a starting point, I believe that his concept of transforming leadership is closer to current conceptions of *transformative leadership* than to the theories of transformational leadership identified earlier. For example, in his 2003 book, *Transforming Leadership*, Burns describes leadership as a moral undertaking whose greatest task "must be to respond to the billions of the world's people in the direst want" (p. 2). He distinguishes between change (substituting one thing for another) and transformation ("a change in the very condition or nature of something," p. 24) and argues against incremental changes that can take lifetimes. Indeed, Burns (1978) thinks of transforming leadership as revolutionary and explains, "Revolution is a complete and pervasive transformation of an entire social system" (p. 202). *Transformative leadership* calls educational leaders to that kind of change.

Transformative leadership, thus, owes its origins to Burns's (1978) discussion of transforming leadership, but some conceptions (e.g., see Anello, Hernandez, & Khadem, 2014) also draw on Mezirow's (1991, 1996) theory of transformative learning. The latter posits the need to effect change in one's frames of reference and to "develop an appreciation of our own culture and the associated privileges and powers" (Taylor, 2006, p. 92). Davis (2006), for example, emphasizes that transformative learning "involves the acquisition (or manipulation) of knowledge that disrupts prior learning and stimulates the reflective reshaping of deeply ingrained knowledge and belief structures" (p. 1). And Anello, Hernandez, and Khadem state, "Transformative learning challenges our ways of thinking and helps us to critically examine the fundamental assumptions underlying our worldview or mental models, resulting in life-changing insights" (p. 3). One can easily see from these few quotations the fundamental differences between leadership theories that continue to see schools as islands, divorced from the socio-political forces surrounding them, and *transformative* theories that reject what Wrigley (2013) calls "moral reductionism whereby researchers can wash their hands of responsibility for the social impact of their work" (p. 37).

Several theories of transformative leadership have emerged from a close examination of the work of Burns and Mezirow, all advocating similar approaches to leading for significant transformation. Further, numerous scholars refer to transformative leadership in their own research and advocacy, without expanding on the term itself. As the need for a radically different approach to educational leadership became apparent, I began an exhaustive quest for a robust leadership theory that foregrounds equity, inclusion, and social justice. As I reviewed all of the available published literature using the term *transformative*, I found references in social science work in South Africa, a number of references in nursing and healthcare administration,

references in curriculum and learning theory, and gradually, mention in educational leadership literature.[4] From all of these sources, I identified what I call eight tenets of transformative leadership:

1. a mandate for deep and equitable change
2. the need to deconstruct knowledge frameworks that perpetuate inequity and injustice and to reconstruct them in more equitable ways
3. the need to address the inequitable distribution of power
4. an emphasis on both private and public (individual and collective) good
5. a focus on emancipation, democracy, equity, and justice
6. an emphasis on interconnectedness, interdependence, and global awareness
7. the necessity of balancing critique with promise
8. the call to exhibit moral courage. (Shields, 2012)

That these tenets are amazingly similar to the steps advanced by Anello, Hernandez, and Khadem (2014), who developed their model independently at Nur University in Boliva, attests, I believe, to the importance and robustness of the concept of transformative leadership. Their model, inspired by the work of Dr. Anello in public health in Bolivia, calls for six steps: "providing context, challenging mental models, transforming our understanding through critical analysis, adopting a new conceptual framework, participating in a learning community, and taking action" (Anello et al., loc. 223). They subsequently sub-divide their "taking action" step into what they call "18 capabilities" organized into the categories of capabilities for personal

---

4 For a more comprehensive history see Shields, C. M. (2010), Leadership: Transformative. In E. Baker, B. McGaw, & P. Peterson (Eds.), *International Encyclopedia of Education* (3rd ed.). Oxford: Elsevier.

transformation, capabilities for transformation of interpersonal relationships, and capabilities for social transformation.

A final model, developed by Caldwell et al. (2012) and published in the *Journal of Business Ethics*, attempts to integrate features of several other leadership theories and then identifies ten clarifying principles. Thus, the authors identify "well-recognized features of six highly regarded leadership perspectives: transformational leadership, charismatic leadership, level 5 leadership, principle-centered leadership, servant leadership, and covenantal leadership" (p. 177). All of these, taken together, support what the authors claim to be "some universal principles and values" (p. 179). Their emphasis on principles and values, as well as both personal and collective transformation, are consistent with the other two approaches identified here.

What is noteworthy, as one examines these and other transformative approaches to leadership, is that they all require thoughtful and critical self-examination, critique of existing mental models and conceptual frameworks, and an action orientation. Moreover, they are complex, reflecting multiple dimensions, tenets, principles, or capabilities that are necessary if organizational transformation is to be achieved. Transformation is never stagnant. Once beliefs have been challenged, new models developed, and actions determined and taken, the work begins again, as depicted in figure 1.3 below.

Figure 1.3. Transformative Leadership Model.

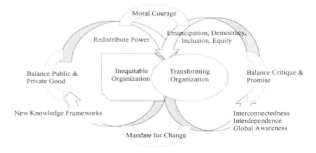

Conscientization is Freire's term for becoming deeply and critically aware in ways that lead to empowerment as well as transformative action.

This model of transformative leadership roughly resembles an infinity symbol in that it contains two continuous and intersecting loops, starting with the inequitable organization (the square) that needs to be transformed into the more inclusive and inviting circle. One moves through the left side of the model, increasing one's conscientization as one examines, challenges, and changes one's deeply held beliefs and assumptions, and identifies the need to address inequitable power relations and to focus on both private and public good. As one moves to the right side of the model, one moves from an emphasis on critique to one of action as we transform pedagogy, policies, and practices to promote emancipation, democracy, equity, and inclusion and to help students understand the interconnectedness and interdependence of the world in which we live. All of this is undergirded at the bottom by the mandate for deep change and connected and held together at the top by the need for moral courage.

The Mandate for Transformative Leadership

Transformative leadership, regardless of the authorship or provenance of the concept, begins with the identification of inequities in the social context of education and recognition of the responsibility of educators. A wide-awake educational leader—who is attentive to all individuals and groups within his or her school—may soon begin to notice inequities in the organizational context, perhaps excessive negative comments or bullying of LGBTQ students, unequal educational outcomes for Latino students, excessive rates of suspension and discipline for African American students, the inability of students living in poverty to participate in field trips, or an apparent lack of involvement of female Muslim students in sports' activities. In these, and many other cases, including inequitable performance on standardized tests, there are very likely underlying social and cultural

assumptions or hegemonic practices within the school that prevent equitable participation and outcomes. The transformative school leader begins with a sense of the urgency of addressing barriers that perpetuate these inequities and hence operates with a clear, non-negotiable mandate for deep and equitable change or transformation.

Tenet 1: Mandate for deep and equitable change. This examination of one's context—both within and beyond the organization—is thus the first tenet I have identified: a mandate for deep and equitable change. Moreover, it is consistent with Anello, Hernandez, and Khadem's model of transformative leadership, in which "providing context" is their first step.

Critique and Challenge

Several of the tenets of transformative leadership require that we both critique and challenge existing beliefs, values, assumptions, structures, and practices. Once inequities have been identified and the burden for change accepted, the transformative leader must delve into the elements that perpetuate inequity.

Tenet 2: Deconstructing and reconstructing knowledge frameworks. In general, this calls for what I have called elsewhere (Shields, 2011, 2013) called "deconstructing knowledge frameworks that perpetuate inequities and reconstructing them in new and more equitable ways." Caldwell et al. (2012) posit, "Transformative leaders seek new solutions that require people to rethink their assumptions, rather than simply returning to old solutions to resolve new problems" (p. 176). And as we have seen, three of the steps identified by Anello et al. (2014) are (1) challenging mental models, (2) transforming our understanding through critical analysis, and (3) adopting a new conceptual framework. Regardless of the terminology, the concepts are identical and call for a critical examination and rethinking of our beliefs and assumptions.

Unless we address the underlying thought patterns that perpetuate discrimination, institutional racism, classism, homophobia, or deficit thinking (to name only a few), reform efforts will fail. This step involves considerable personal reflection and critique as well as admitting that some of what we have learned and believed is actually wrong. It then requires transformative leaders to help others to engage in similar difficult examinations of acquired and sometimes deeply entrenched beliefs and practices.

Jumping too quickly to a new program or a new policy without first challenging and changing existing inappropriate and incorrect norms will be counterproductive. Anello et al. agree, saying, "Unless we scrutinize our mental models critically and unemotionally with the goal of finding the flaws in our thinking, we cannot make the learning leap to a new and more profound level of understanding" (loc. 263). If our own tacit assumptions are that children who come from poverty are less able to learn than middle-class children, no remedial reading or math program will counteract the force of our beliefs and students' perceptions of our underlying lack of confidence in their capacity to perform. If the conventional wisdom with which we have grown up is that LGBTQ students' lifestyles are immoral or unnatural and that these students might "contaminate" or negatively influence others, until we confront this perception, we will be unable to rectify the hostile school climate that is a factor in their behavior, self-confidence, and academic achievement.

Tenet 3: Redistributing the inequitable distribution of power. Careful examination of the factors inhibiting the full participation and inclusion of all will likely also result in a new understanding of the power inequities related to how certain policies or practices are perpetuated. Oakes and Rogers (2006) assert,

Merely documenting inequality will not, in and of itself, lead to more adequate and equitable

schooling. Straightforward and obvious claims of injustice can be transformed, in the hands of lawyers, researchers, and policymakers, into highly technical disputes about statistical methods or esoteric debates about motivational theories. Scientific and technical arguments have a limited capacity to resolve matters that reach so deeply into cultural values and political contention. (p. 13)

Clearly this is an accurate statement, given how long income and wage disparities have been well documented but unaddressed in this country. In part this is because people do not want to give up what they perceive to be in their own interest. The adage attributed to Lord Acton that power corrupts and absolute power corrupts absolutely is, indeed, too often accurate. Moreover it finds its expression in the perpetuation of decision-making methods and structures that, once again, privilege those who already have power and fail to include new and more diverse values and perspectives.

In 2003, Weiner defined transformative leadership with reference to power saying, "Transformative leadership is an exercise of power and authority that begins with questions of justice, democracy, and the dialectic between individual accountability and social responsibility" (p. 89). In his examination of the career of Paulo Freire as Secretary of Education in Brazil between 1989 and 1991, he writes,

As Freire's administration and position as Secretariat suggest, leadership, authority and power become transformative when they are directed towards the service of emancipating systemically entrenched attitudes, behaviors, and ideas, as well as instigating structural transformations at a material level. (p. 93)

Transforming power to use it in the service of emancipation and structural change is the concept described in the third tenet as "the need to address

the inequitable distribution of power" and is a necessary component of the critical reflection and reconceptualization required for transformation of knowledge frameworks.

Emancipatory Goals

After one has identified the underlying bases for inequities in organizational structures, practices, and policies, transformative leaders will reflect on the fact that too often the status quo is perpetuated in both policy and pedagogical practice. When transformative educational leaders recognize the important role education plays in advancing the public good and in supporting the development and improvement of our democratic society, they must reorient policy, curriculum, and pedagogy to focus on emancipation, democracy, equity, and justice.

It must be asserted forcefully here that *transformative leadership* is not only a theory for a more just and equitable learning environment; it also undergirds and enables all other changes aimed at reducing or eliminating the "achievement gap" between dominant culture and minoritized students. If we do not remove barriers to learning, children will remain unable to concentrate on the task at hand. If we do not equalize the inputs, outputs, and outcomes of education, those who have been marginalized will continue to hover on the outside; those who have been confined and oppressed by current systems will never find emancipation.

Tenet 4: Emphasis on both public and private good. To ensure that education supports both individual advancement and the welfare of a deeply democratic society, it is important to recognize that it comprises both public and private good. Given the current focus on what is sometimes known as "college and career readiness," this tenet requires significant change in the ways in which we have come to think about the goals and purposes of education. A recent publication from the U.S.

Department of Education sets forth the expectation that funding will be tied to "state-developed standards in English language arts and mathematics that build toward college and career readiness by the time students graduate from high school" (USDE, 2010, p. 2). The booklet includes a section titled "Why Focus on College and Career Readiness?" in which the discussion explains that too many students have to enroll in remedial courses in college and that too many employers believe students are ill prepared for the workforce when they graduate from high school. Although these statements are accurate, nowhere in the publication does one also find reference to "society," "democracy," or "public good."

This is consistent with historian David Labaree's (1997) argument that education's emphasis has changed from a focus on preparing citizens to one in which education has become a commodity. He writes that education has "increasingly come to be perceived as a private good that is harnessed to the pursuit of personal advantage; and, on the whole, the consequences of this for both school and society have been profoundly negative" (p. 43). In this private good, education is seen as a means of acquiring a credential, a way of acquiring a better position, and as a proving ground for a market ideal rather than as a means of acquiring knowledge or of citizenship training. Success or failure is thus attributed solely to an individual's effort and achievement with no thought given to barriers or supports offered by social structures. In contrast, Labaree defines public good as "one where benefits are enjoyed by all the members of the community, whether or not they actually contributed to the production of this good" (p. 51); he offered examples of goods such as "police protection, street maintenance, public parks, open-air sculpture, and air pollution control" (p. 51).

The increasing emphasis on private goods may also be associated with the current attacks on public schools and arguments directed at removing

public control and privatizing education, including the expansive and rapid growth of the charter school movement and "for-profit" academies. The consequence, therefore, is one seen increasingly and particularly in the largest and most challenged urban areas in this country—the abandonment of public education by all but the poorest of citizens and the abject learning environments remaining for those who cannot afford (for reasons of time, transportation, or other resources) to choose otherwise.

Democratic public education is the crucible of a strong civil society. Excellent public schools are necessary to safeguard the opportunities of those who cannot, or do not, for whatever reason, opt to move away from a neighborhood school. Moreover, in a democracy, all students should rightfully experience equitable educational opportunities for both personal development and for full participation in our democratic society. Unfortunately, this is not the case. When one finds disparities in per pupil funding within a state such that urban school per pupil funding is less than half that of more wealthy suburban districts,[5] something is wrong.

Tenet 5: A focus on emancipation, democracy, equity, and justice. This overarching goal is reflected in transformative leadership's fifth tenet and demands that we consider how to create an organization in which all members—teachers, non-academic staff, students, and parents—not only feel welcome and included in organizational life but also in which the practices of the organization are grounded in principles of democracy, equity, justice, and emancipation. I use the term *emancipation* instead of the more commonly used *freedom*, because freedom too often has come to be interpreted, in our neo-liberal society, as the ability to pursue individual goals without interference, external control, or regulation that may impose constraints. Hence, choice in

Emancipation requires action on the part of those who hold others captive; it implies empowerment that enables everyone to fully participate in all aspects of civil life.

---

5   At minimum, this is the case in Illinois and Michigan; it is likely the case in many other states as well.

education is often associated with freedom—one's ability to choose for oneself the appropriate school for one's child. Emancipation, however, implies something more active, suggesting that those who have been excluded, marginalized, or inhibited by certain policies or practices are now liberated to fully participate in what Green (1999) calls "a *deeper conception of democracy* that expresses the experience-based possibility of more equal, respectful, and mutually beneficial ways of community life" (p. vi).

This tenet, therefore, emphasizes the mutual benefit of being involved in a particular school or institution. It is not sufficient for some, or even most, to enjoy working there, to succeed academically, to have their voices heard. Instead, the goal of democracy and emancipation is clarified by the addition of the words *equity* and *justice*. In other words, the transformative leader works to create a learning environment in which each member feels welcome, valued, and included. These emancipatory goals are reflective of Astin and Astin's (2000) vision for transformative leadership and social change:

> We believe that the value ends of leadership should be to enhance equity, social justice, and the quality of life; to expand access and opportunity; to encourage respect for difference and diversity; to strengthen democracy, civic life, and civic responsibility; and to promote cultural enrichment, creative expression, intellectual honesty, the advancement of knowledge, and personal freedom coupled with responsibility. (p. 11)

Unfortunately, this description is not applicable to life in many educational organizations today.

Transformative Action

Moving from recognition of inequity, even changing one's deeply held assumptions and beliefs, is difficult and time-consuming work. Yet one cannot

move to actions that will successfully promote and sustain organizational transformation without critical reflection and understanding. As will be discussed in more detail in subsequent chapters, to accomplish the creation of new mental models and knowledge frameworks requires moral courage. Moral courage stresses the need to be open to admitting one is wrong, to changing one's mind; hence, to a sense of discomfort, uncertainty, and ambiguity. Alexander Sidorkin emphasizes the role of dialogue—both internal and with others—in helping one reach new understandings. In fact, he argues that educators need to learn the importance of listening to an internal questioning and doubting dialogue. His point is that "a fully consistent message simply does not capture the complexity of moral life" (2002, p. 156). For example, I can firmly commit myself to having all students pass the required standardized tests, but at the same time reject practices that may narrow the curriculum by focusing on test preparation and rote learning. I can admit that I might be uncertain should my child reflect a desire for gender transformation surgery, while at the same time fiercely defending the need for gender neutral washrooms in my child's school.

Recognizing the difference, as does Burns (2003), between *change* and *transformation* undergirds the transformative action called for in this and the remaining three tenets of transformative leadership. Burns states that change is simply to "substitute one thing for another" (p. 24) as is so often the case in education when one reading or math program is substituted for another, or when one principal is relieved of his or her duties only to be replaced with another with a similar mindset and training. On the other hand, Burns describes transformation as

> a metamorphosis in form or structure, a change in the very condition or nature of a thing, ... a radical change ... as when a frog is transformed into a prince or a carriage maker into an auto factory. (p. 24)

Only this kind of transformation can truly result in the emancipation, democratization, equity, and justice required for our educational organizations to truly serve all individuals as well as our democracy as a whole.

Tenet 6: Emphasis on interconnectedness, interdependence, and global awareness. Unless we begin to take seriously tenet 6, the trend to more privatization of education identified in tenet 4 is likely to continue. Moreover, the focus on emancipation, democracy, equity, and justice will seem nationalistic and self-serving instead of preparing students for citizenship, not only in a nation but throughout the world. Too often, we have failed to recognize our mutual dependence and interdependence. We have lost our sense of responsibility for one another—of being our brother's keeper. And we do so at our peril.

In recent years, with the rise of the Occupy movement, there has been an increased focus on those who hold the top 1% of wealth. In May 2011, economist Joseph Stiglitz wrote in *Vanity Fair:*

> In our democracy, 1% of the people take nearly a quarter of the nation's income ... In terms of wealth rather than income, the top 1% control 40% ... [as a result] the top 1% have the best houses, the best educations, the best doctors, and the best lifestyles, but there is one thing that money doesn't seem to have bought: an understanding that their fate is bound up with how the other 99% live. Throughout history, this is something that the top 1% eventually do learn. Too late.

His closing comment is telling. The fate of the wealthy is bound up with how the other 99% live. The fate of those in the suburbs is bound up with how those in the hearts of our cities live; the fate of those of us who live in North America is bound up with how those in Nepal, Bangladesh, Togo, or China live.

What does all of this have to do with American students and why does it matter? Events that occur

elsewhere affect us all. The increase in human trafficking resulting from the neglect of refugees reaches to America. Demand for illegal drugs in the United States has been associated with the "more than 47,000 unaccompanied migrant children from Central America who were apprehended by US Border Patrol agents during the previous eight months" (Cáceres, 2014, p. 1). In 2012, Americans sent a staggering $120 billion plus to families abroad, thus helping developing economies elsewhere (Tomlinson, 2013), keeping people employed, reducing illegal immigration, and enhancing everyone's purchasing power. At the same time, some decry the loss of so much money that could circulate in the U.S. economy.

Regardless of one's ideological position, it is important for students to reflect on, to discuss, and to debate these and many other issues that not only have worldwide import but that also impact how we live together at home.

Tenet 7: Balance critique with promise. To take the kind of transformative action reflected in tenets 5 and 6 requires both critique and action that fulfills not only individual excellence but also the promise of a better world. If our educative goal is transformation of the social, cultural, and economic inequities throughout the world and the increased well-being and respect of all human beings, we must know what is occurring elsewhere in the world. We must critique the many policies at home and abroad that result in human suffering and despair and we must take action. This requires transformative educators to be critical and curious citizens, asking the same questions of governmental policies that we ask of decisions in our schools: who is marginalized, excluded, disadvantaged by a given decision and who is privileged, included, and advantaged?

Acknowledging that there is a gap in educational achievement between Black, Caucasian, Indigenous, and Latino students is one thing. Determining to take action to change the outcome

> Promise, as both a noun and a verb, involves a sense of contract as well as the fulfillment of that contract. It implies a commitment to action that will lead to better opportunities and greater inclusion and equity for all.

is something else. Challenging deficit beliefs, changing the instructional program, reallocating resources, including personnel—all are required if significant transformation is to be achieved. Alone, adopting a new program will do little. Placing a different, more experienced teacher with a small group of struggling students may help but only if the beliefs and values of both the teacher and the program are consistent with high expectations and empowerment.

The point of transformative leadership is to make decisions and take actions that not only benefit all students but that offer support, inclusion, equity, and, hence, hope and promise to the most marginalized. Critique in this sense comes from what is often known as critical theory or critical perspectives. The *Stanford Encyclopedia of Philosophy* (2005) explains:

> a "critical" theory may be distinguished from a "traditional" theory according to a specific practical purpose: a theory is critical to the extent that it seeks human "emancipation from slavery", acts as a "liberating ... influence," and works "to create a world which satisfies the needs and powers" of human beings (Horkheimer 1972, 246) ... In both the broad and the narrow senses, however, a critical theory provides the descriptive and normative bases for social inquiry aimed at decreasing domination and increasing freedom in all their forms.

The key is purpose—and it is precisely the specific practical purpose that helps to differentiate transformative leadership from other leadership theories. A critical theory aims at doing exactly that: increasing freedom and reducing domination of students who have not normally found a fully inclusive and empowering learning environment in their schools. Thus, critical transformative leadership both recognizes the barriers and takes action aimed at redress of what Maxine Greene termed society's "unfulfilled promises" (1998). For

that reason, critique and promise must go hand in hand.

Impetus for Transformation

The impetus for transformation is to be found in the last tenet of transformative leadership.

Tenet 8: Exhibit moral courage. Some have argued that moral courage should be placed at the beginning, as the first tenet of transformative leadership, in that courage is required throughout. However, once one has seen the extent of the necessary transformation—personal, professional, organizational, cultural, structural, and pedagogical, the necessity for moral courage becomes even more obvious. For that reason, and recognizing that moral courage must infuse all aspects of significant transformation, I place it here.

Taking the time to reflect on one's own beliefs is the starting point. Even there, acknowledging one's biases and prejudices and changing the way one thinks or talks takes courage. Raising contentious issues, like racism or homophobia, that perpetuate domination and social advantage takes courage. Eliminating practices that advantage some students to the exclusion of others takes courage. There will be opposition; there will be pushback; and there will be criticism (not critique). Weiner (2003) argues,

> Transformative leadership, to be transformative, must confront more than just what is, and work toward creating an alternative political and social imagination that does not rest solely on the rule of capital or the hollow moralism of neoconservatives, but is rooted in radical democratic struggle. (p. 97)

He goes on to state that transformative leadership also

> implies the necessity to link not only the private and public, but also the empirical and theoretical,

the everyday and the future, the imaginative and the real, the past and the forgotten, history and tradition, power and knowledge, and learning and life. (p. 98)

These activities are not the traditional actions associated with school leaders as can be seen by the courses still emphasized by so many leadership preparation programs: economics, the role of the principal, school improvement, instructional leadership, education law. Each of these, as most often taught, still focuses on the more technical, rational, and transactional aspects of leadership. Moreover, while useful, they do not comprise a transformative approach to leading organizations that are still, for the most part, fraught with inequities and dominated by privilege.

As we have seen, transformative educational leadership is first and foremost a way of life. The theory comprises a set of principles or tenets that are not prescriptive but instead undergird everything a leader thinks or does. These principles ground leadership practice in decisions that are not only ethical but also socially just, focusing always on overcoming domination and prejudice, on enhancing liberation, and on creating the conditions for emancipation, empowerment, and full participation.

Looking Ahead

In this chapter, I have described some of the reasons why I believe a new, more equitable, more inclusive, and more socially transformative theory of leadership is required for our schools and educational organizations. I have begun to outline some of the inequities and unfulfilled promises of our current social and educational systems. I have made the case for the need for Tenet 1: the mandate for deep and equitable change. In Chapter 2, as we focus primarily on Tenet 2, I shall elaborate some

of the beliefs, values, and assumptions that under-gird successful transformation, clarify some elements of educational organizations that need to be deconstructed, and some beliefs that must be challenged. I will identify ways in which new mental models and frameworks must be constructed if true transformation is to be the result.

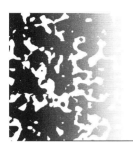

Critique, Challenge, Deconstruction, and Reconstruction

Gabriel lived with his four siblings in relative comfort in Managua, Nicaragua, until the Sandinista regime targeted his family, killing two uncles and confiscating everything his parents had worked so hard to build. Ultimately the decision was made for his father to give up his engineering job, his mother to sacrifice her hair salon, and for the family to seek refuge in Florida. Gabriel recalls, "We escaped on foot; I remember my dad holding me so tightly as he carried me across the river." After weeks on the road, they finally arrived in Miami, Florida, to join relatives who had immigrated previously. He explains, "My father worked three jobs, mostly washing dishes, because that was the only work he could find. He never slept, I mean he worked so hard just to put food on the table; we were so poor. We lived in a one-bedroom apartment, all of us slept in one room. But, somehow, my mom and dad always found a way to provide for us."

Gabriel entered primary school as an English language learner. Due to his lack of English proficiency,

he was soon tracked into a self-contained learning disabled (LD) classroom, where he languished unceremoniously for nearly a decade. He explained, "I didn't really think school was that hard; the teachers didn't really care about giving us much homework; they all thought we were LD and couldn't learn anyway. I didn't have to try that hard, I mean the teachers didn't really expect much of us." At the same time, Gabriel had developed a passion for computers and acquired enough proficiency that he was able to recite long strings of computer code, link whole apartment buildings to a single Internet connection, and restore crashed systems in a matter of minutes; nonetheless, neither he nor his teachers recognized this as an indication of his cognitive ability.

Just before his 16th birthday, Gabriel walked into an inner-city Social Security office, looking for a part-time job to help support his impoverished family. He was seriously considering dropping out of school, because, in his words, he was "not smart enough to graduate." Fortunately, one of the young men working in the office recognized Gabriel's potential and spent many months working with him, encouraging him, insisting that he resist using self-deprecating labels, and patiently inspiring him to work through challenging problems. Finally Gabriel began to realize that he "was not dumb," and summoned his courage to talk to his 10th grade teacher who fought with the dean of the school to convince him to move Gabriel to a regular class despite his low test scores.

Following two years of night school and summer school, and "tons of homework," Gabriel walked proudly across the stage to accept his regular diploma. Subsequently, he completed a degree in computer science and now works as a network administrator for a luxury hotel chain. In April 2015, while I was attending an academic conference in Chicago, his mentor introduced me to Gabriel, who was overseeing the red carpet opening of a deluxe downtown hotel.

In Chapter 1, I referred to Maxine Green's (1998) belief that we live in a society of unfulfilled

promises and to the need to develop what Freire (1970) called "conscientization"—a heightened awareness and understanding of the circumstances of others. In educational *transformative leadership*, after one has examined the context and accepted the mandate for deep and equitable change, the second tenet focuses on beliefs, values, assumptions, and practices that perpetuate inequity and therefore need to be deconstructed. Then the task is to create new knowledge frameworks that are more equitable, inclusive, and socially just.

All eight tenets of *transformative leadership* work together to create more inclusive, equitable, and socially just schools (and ultimately societies); they are interactive, relatively non-hierarchical, and inextricably interconnected. To that end, a transformative leader attends to all components of the theory. Nevertheless, it is important to spend enough time considering Tenet 2, **the need to deconstruct knowledge frameworks that perpetuate inequity and to reconstruct them in more equitable ways.** It is essential to examine our own underlying beliefs, assumptions, and mental models, and then to lead others in the organization to do the same, if significant and sustained transformation is to occur. As previously noted, in the Bolivian conception of transformative leadership offered by Anello, Hernandez, and Khadem (2014), the concept of reconstructing mental models is seen as so important that it comprises three distinct stages: challenging mental models, transforming our understanding through critical analysis, and adopting a new conceptual framework.

Too often, I have seen people adopt what they claim to be a transformative approach, but then move too quickly to new programs, policies, or pedagogies without first transforming understanding. As we shall see as we further examine the predominance of *deficit thinking*, as one framework that must be deconstructed, if we do not change educators' beliefs about minoritized children's

> Deconstruction involves more than simply challenging or discussing what currently exists. As in the field of building construction, it actually involves dismantling and tearing down one way of thinking and replacing it with new and more appropriate frameworks.

capacities and abilities, then regardless of what else may change, we continue to convey both covert and overt messages that school is not for them and that they do not really belong. Thus, they will continue to struggle on the margins of our pedagogical practices.

The story of Gabriel, with which this chapter opens, clearly demonstrates a number of negative and unfortunate assumptions, beliefs, and practices that will be discussed further in this chapter. The challenges he faced, from the Sandinistas killing his uncles, to his refugee status, to being an English Language Learner misplaced in a class for learning-disabled children—were clearly not of his making. He was lucky eventually to find an adult who believed in him, who supported and encouraged him, and helped him to advocate for himself. This must not be the luck of the draw. His teachers made numerous assumptions about him and about his family, but they were wrong. Had they taken the time to get to know him, to understand why his parents did not get to the school for parent-teacher meetings, to connect his skill with computers to the possibility of ability in other areas, then his experience might have been different.

A Society of Unfulfilled Promise

The notion of challenging mental models is reminiscent of a poster I once found which read, "Don't believe everything you think." In other words, we acquire beliefs and assumptions over time from our parents, our society, our culture, and the many messages with which we are bombarded from birth from spoken, visual, and print media. The more we express these perspectives, the more we come to believe them, failing to reflect on whether or not they represent the best available "truth." Among others, we acquire what some have called "-obias and -isms"—homophobia, Islamophobia, racism,

sexism, classism, and many more. All of these beliefs comprise the ways in which we think about the world in which we live and about others with whom we come in contact. They tell us what behaviors, words, and ideological positions are acceptable, as well as what are inappropriate and undesirable.

Bourdieu described the totality of these beliefs as our "habitus," explaining that habitus represents a

> system of durable, transposable dispositions, structured structures predisposed to function as structuring structures, that is, as principles which generate and organize practices and representations that can be objectively adapted to their outcomes without presupposing a conscious aiming at ends or an express mastery of the operations necessary to attain them. (Swartz, 1997, p. 101)

This rather convoluted explanation suggests that our dispositions and understandings are so deeply ingrained that they constitute structures that organize and perpetuate societal norms often at a subconscious level. Because we rarely question these understandings, our habitus may have come to represent hegemonic beliefs and practices, marginalizing some and privileging others. Swartz states that Bourdieu thinks of "school systems as the institutionalized context where the intellectual habitus of a culture develops" (p. 102). This makes our task critically important. For if school systems do not help individuals and communities to understand the ways in which culture preserves certain norms, and to challenge the norms that perpetuate inequity and inequality, then little meaningful change will occur.

Conscientization

The process begins with oneself—with "conscientization," as an individual comes to better know and understand his or her own lived experiences and those of others, and to realize, often with considerable discomfort, the part one has played in the

perpetuation of unfulfilled promises. In fact, too often our practices refute the opening words of the U.S. Declaration of Independence:

> We hold these truths to be self-evident, that all men are created equal, that they are endowed by their Creator with certain unalienable Rights, that among these are Life, Liberty and the pursuit of Happiness. That to secure these rights, Governments are instituted among Men.

Regrettably, the truths have not been, nor are they still, self-evident or others would not experience so many barriers to their ability to live in security and safety and to pursue happiness. Moreover, our governments, including their educational institutions, have not fulfilled their promise of securing these rights.

As transformative leaders begin to deconstruct inequitable and incorrect knowledge frameworks and to reconstruct them in more inclusive and socially just ways, we must learn to locate ourselves. We can no longer act as though we all share a lived reality that is generally experienced and understood. As a third generation university-educated White, straight woman, from a family of professionals, I must locate myself as coming from privilege. Yet, even as I benefit from "White privilege," I do not have to choose it. I can empathize with those whose experience is different; I can stand beside them I can work to overcome the barriers that my privilege has erected for them; and I can work *with* them to create transformation. But I must acknowledge that my position makes me complicit. I benefit from the dominant culture in ways of which I likely remain partially unaware. Only as I am authentic, locating myself in my privilege, can I work in solidarity with those whose experience is vastly different from mine.[1]

> Whiteness or White privilege refers to the entire social system that has been constructed and developed by White colonial power in hegemonic ways. It refers to the system from which (mostly) White people continue to benefit at the expense of others. It does not automatically refer to skin color but to an unquestioning acceptance and perpetuation of the benefits of inequity.

---

1   The outrage, during the summer of 2015, at the discovery that activist Rachel Dolezal was not Black is a case

Wynne (2015) states that she begins almost every public talk with the following words: "The United States is a racist country and because of that, I, as a white person, am the beneficiary of power and privileges that have an adverse effect on citizens of color" (p. 363). This perspective is consistent with one advocated by Gloria Ladson-Billings in her keynote address upon receipt of the 2015 Social Justice in Education Award. In response to a question following her address, she replied that "being white is a moral choice," one I do not have to take on. Thus, she described "Whiteness" as a floating signifier, a political project, and one we either choose to be part of or reject. This is a difficult concept and one that few educators have either encountered or made their own, yet self-location is an essential starting point. It permits us to reject the "missionary stance" and to act in solidarity, without pretending to have experienced or to truly understand the Other's pain and lived experience. It avoids pretense and provides an explicit starting point for both dialogue and for working together.

Once leaders have begun to reconstruct their own belief systems based on both self-reflection and deep dialogue with others, they begin to discover more robust truths that can lead to more equitable practices. It then becomes a moral imperative to help others to do the same. The deconstruction of deeply entrenched beliefs and assumptions is both psychological and sociological as one examines one's own upbringing and values and those of the organization in which one exercises leadership. Organizational beliefs are more than simply the sum of what the individuals within them believe at a point in time. They also comprise all of the firmly ingrained historical and

---

in point. Unfortunately her dissimulation and lies have destroyed much, if not all, of the good work she has done. Honestly locating herself could have avoided the entire furor.

cultural beliefs that have made up the "habitus" of education over time. The examination, therefore, often needs to include the traditions, values, and practices that have been passed down over time and that comprise the culture of the organization. This becomes particularly difficult when it appears necessary to understand, honor, and respect the traditions of the past, while, at the same time, challenging areas where inequities appear.

Habitus also helps to explain why beliefs and values are so robust and so difficult to change; they have been developed over time and have become part of the normal, accepted, and acceptable operation of the organization. One example I experienced personally when working at the University of Illinois was the highly controversial and divisive challenge to the university's long-standing mascot, Chief Illiniwek. More recent examples include the changing of the name of Squaw Island near Buffalo, New York, to Unity Island; the change from Mount McKinley back to the original Denali; and the recently increased consciousness of the racist history and symbolism of the Confederate flag and its removal from several public places in southern states. Less obvious and more challenging examples that may need to be reconsidered arise from cultures in which woman are not permitted to speak in public or in particular traditional ceremonies or spaces.

21st Century Inequities: Creating New Frameworks

It would be impossible in a small primer to identify and explore all of the unfair assumptions and inequitable practices that perpetuate social exclusion and educational inequity. However, there are some obvious starting points that pertain to almost every community and school across the nation. Here I will explore the concepts related to deficit thinking, racism, sexual orientation and gender identity,

social class and poverty, language and ethnicity, and religious freedom. The intent is to demonstrate unequivocally why these persistent issues must be explored, understood, and challenged; how they perpetuate inequities in our schools; and why they must be reconstructed in more socially just ways. I begin by presenting a metaphor that clearly illustrates, using a familiar game, why we need to think differently about schooling and the society in which it is embedded.

A Game of Monopoly: A Metaphor

A friend of mine recently explained social justice by referring to the well-known game of Monopoly. Imagine that you and a few friends have been playing the game for an hour, and that most of the properties have been purchased and many have already been developed with houses or hotels. Suddenly Gabriel and Jamail arrive and ask to join the game. "Sure," one friend responds, shaking the dice for her turn, "pull up a chair." But the newcomers hesitate, and tentatively ask if you would be willing to start again or to redistribute some of the already acquired properties and wealth. None of the current players responds, and the play continues. Finally, someone hands the dice to one of the newcomers, saying, "Here, it's your turn." Reluctantly, Gabriel rolls the dice, and lands on a fully developed purple property. He asks again, "Could we start again so Jamail and I can have a chance?" But none of the current players is willing to give up the advantages already gained.

It is readily apparent to anyone familiar with the game that the simple act of permitting others to join the game is not adequate. Unless wealth and property are redistributed, nothing the newcomers do will result in success. In fact, they will quickly become frustrated as their options are reduced to paying rent, falling into bankruptcy,

going to jail, or dropping out of the game once again.[2]

In many ways, this is a metaphor for our highly stratified and deeply unjust society. Transformative educators will need to act deliberately and consistently to effect change. They will need to address personal prejudices as well as institutionalized racism and discrimination, inequitable power elites, inadequate facilities, and so on. And they will need to find ways to redistribute resources so everyone can "play." Of course this is easier said than done. A quarter century ago, scholar Lisa Delpit (1989) wrote about how every organization is characterized by rules of power. Moreover, she argued, those who have the power are the least aware of how it operates to marginalize and exclude others. Similarly it is difficult to understand, at first, how one's own deeply held beliefs might prevent an inclusive, equitable, and socially just learning environment for some. Yet, if those who already had the advantage in the Monopoly game had stopped, even briefly, to consider the situation of Gabriel and Jamail, they would have begun to understand the necessity of redistributing what was already held; that is, if they truly wanted them to be able to play on an equal footing.

> Equity is not synonymous with equality. The latter assumes sameness of treatment for everyone, while the former assumes differential inputs to effect similar outcomes and outputs.

However, as Oakes and Rogers (2006) and others point out, simply seeing the inequities does not necessarily result in equitable change. The reasons for this are complex and debated by some of the world's most prominent scholars of human behaviors. Here we will simply state the obvious. We may not want to give everyone an equal chance, assuming that opportunity is a zero sum game and that, as in the Monopoly game, if we increase the advantage to some, it will decrease our own advantage. It is definitely not easy to convince people to give up

---

2   I subsequently found a striking image called "Black Monopoly" that dramatically supports this analysis by having each square labelled, "Go to jail." It can be found when one searches "image Black Monopoly."

something they perceive is to their advantage to retain. Somehow the moral imperative of all being created equal is not enough; however, the practical recognition that the suffering of some affects the well-being of all may be a pragmatic starting point. Taking the more ethical position and recognizing our interdependence and acknowledging that the well-being of our nation and our world depends on increased equity and inclusion would be an even better moral choice.

Here I want to discuss some of the entrenched beliefs that may need to be challenged, deconstructed, and reconstructed within educational organizations in order for socially just transformation to occur. These include the general category of deficit thinking (which may include both individual and institutional beliefs and practices), as well as the familiar but too rarely addressed issues of race, class, gender identity, and religious belief. These are the beliefs from which we often convey the message to some children that school is not for the likes of them. Almost from day one, we ask questions, give assignments, assume prior knowledge, and engage in practices that exclude some children and privilege others. We ask children to talk or write about their summer vacation or what they did on the weekend, failing to recognize the embarrassment this may cause to some. We encourage participation in fund raising, asking children, for example, to sell subscriptions to magazines, without realizing that some live in tenement houses in which magazine subscriptions would be considered a luxury. And we make assumptions about the educational support provided by parents when they are unable to take unpaid time off work to attend a student-led conference or their child's school performance.

Only when one has carefully considered each of these issues can one move to address the distribution of power that perpetuates these inequities (to be discussed in Chapter 3) as well as pedagogy,

> Deficit thinking is a way of thinking that equates difference with deficiency and that allocates blame for differential outcomes on individuals rather than on systems and institutions.

instruction, and policies, including ability group-
ing, discipline, or homework that will be addressed
in Chapter 4.

Deficit Thinking

There is little debate that mental models help to
explain why some groups of people remain in subordinate positions, excluded from full participation in
the social, political, economic, and cultural organizations and practices of our society. Most often, we
tend to allocate blame or responsibility to the individuals within the designated group, and to ignore
the institutional and societal barriers that have been
erected over time. In other words, we "blame the
victims," arguing that they are lazy, unmotivated,
don't care, don't understand delayed gratification,
have not worked hard enough, and so on.

I recently discussed the contentious nature of
Detroit's public education with a neighbor whose
"solution" was to "take all the children from their
homes and build more boarding schools because
the parents don't care; they can't help!" This is the
kind of comment that allocates all the responsibility
for perceived or real failure on the parents and families and ignores the negative economic situation of
Detroit, the lack of employment and transportation,
the housing policies that perpetuate segregation,
poverty and homelessness, and the failure of schools
to adequately educate all children.

Valencia (1997) explains deficit thinking this
way:

> The deficit thinking paradigm, as a whole, posits
> that students who fail in school do so because of
> alleged internal deficiencies (such as cognitive
> and/or motivational limitations) or shortcomings
> socially linked to the youngster—such as familial
> deficits and dysfunctions. (p. xi)

Valencia goes on to argue that allocating the
responsibility for failure within students and their

families holds "blameless" societal and systemic factors. It also holds blameless societal myths and conceptions that must be changed. Moreover, given that we tend to fear what we do not know, we mentally construct negative images of those who are in some way different from ourselves in order to justify our fear. The next step is often to pathologize difference, believing it is abnormal in some way, and hence something we need to "fix," to eradicate, to cure, instead of a quality to be understood and possibly even valued. Shields, Bishop, and Mazawi (2005) define it this way:

> Pathologizing is a process where perceived structural-functional, cultural, or epistemological deviation from an assumed normal state is ascribed to another group as a product of power relationships, whereby the less powerful group is deemed to be abnormal in some way. Pathologizing is a mode of colonization used to govern, regulate, manage, marginalize, or minoritize primarily through hegemonic discourses. (p. ix)

One example of difference being pathologized rather than accepted, understood, and valued is that of homosexuality, which, until 1973, was listed in the *Diagnostic and Statistical Manual of Psychological Disorders* (DSM), of the American Psychological Association, as a "mental disorder." Although not everyone has yet rejected this position, the scientific evidence is compelling. Moreover, regardless of whether difference is a choice or simply a genetic "condition," each person deserves to be valued and respected, and not pathologized.

In general, deficit thinking is a way of abrogating our responsibility and assigning the blame for failure to those who are, in some way, different from ourselves. It is convenient to argue, for example, that everyone should be treated equally, and to believe that if a policy results in unequal outcomes, it is the fault of people who have not tried hard enough or been adequately motivated to

succeed. But it is important to recall the often-circulated images[3] of three children trying to see over a fence, often labeled "equality" and "justice."

Figure 2.1. Equality or Justice?

Equality   **Justice**

In the equality image, no amount of struggling will permit the child on the right to see over the fence if each has only one similarly sized box. Regardless of how much each wants to see the game, the "level playing field" of one box each simply perpetuates his inability to watch the game. On the other hand, as depicted in the "justice" image, having the taller child on the left actually give up his box and redistribute it to the child on the right, permits all three to successfully accomplish their purpose which, in this case, is to watch the game.

Deficit thinking would suggest it is the fault of the boy on the right that he is not tall enough, that his legs are not long enough, and that he is simply not trying hard enough because he does not really care about seeing the game. This ludicrous situation

---

3   These pictures, which I accessed at https://www.linkedin.com/pulse/equality-doesnt-equal-justice-dave-bennett, seem to be public domain images found in multiple places on the Internet. They are described as "three boys-trying to view a game" and although there is no reason to assume all are boys, I maintain the male pronouns in this discussion.

reminds me of the myth of Procrustes, the mythological Greek innkeeper, who promised each guest a gourmet meal and an excellent night's sleep in a bed that fit him perfectly. Following the evening meal, as guests retired to their room, if they happened to be too short for their bed, he stretched them (Procrustes actually means "the stretcher"), and if they were too tall, he cut off their legs. This one size fits all approach is illustrated in the "Equality" image and is, unfortunately, too often the approach taken in schools. Deficit thinking might imply, with Procrustes, that the "cure" is to simply stretch the child, ensuring he fits the mold of what is perceived as "normal." When we discuss these images in this way, this position is ridiculous, but in schools and social organizations throughout the country, we take similar positions, requiring all children to fit the "schooling" mold rather than adapting schools to meet the needs of changing and diverse populations of children. Often, when confronted with these images, educators complain that the tallest child will then be disadvantaged, because he too needs to learn. And of course, that is true, but he does not need the box in order to attain his goals as demonstrated by the metaphor of "watching the game." He is fully able to do so without the box.

The need to reverse this kind of thinking is incontrovertible. If we continue to blame the child on the right, telling him he is just too short and is not trying hard enough to grow, he will soon internalize the negative message and give up, knowing there is little he can do to change his height. Further, the need to eliminate deficit thinking in education is well documented (Shields, Bishop, & Mazawi, 2005; Valencia, 1997, 2010). In fact, two decades ago, Wagstaff and Fusarelli (1995) found that the *single* most important factor in the academic achievement of minoritized students is the leader's explicit rejection of deficit thinking.

This is because when children are repeatedly being given the message that they cannot learn, or that something is wrong with them or their family,

it is difficult for them to concentrate or to take the formal curriculum very seriously. Expecting Gabriel to work at his age and grade level, while worrying about his family and learning English, may have been unrealistic. But keeping him in an LD class even while asking him to fix his teachers' computers was unconscionable.

Moreover, there is considerable research in education about the value of diverse learning contexts. Children from poverty are more successful if they are educated in schools with more affluent children (Warren, Thompson, & Saegert, 2001). Children who speak more than one language tend to perform better on standardized tests (Lindholm-Leary, 2001). Children who are educated in diverse contexts demonstrate more empathy than those who have only experienced homogeneous contexts.

Transformative educators must take this tenet seriously. Deconstructing deficit thinking and reconstructing the ways in which we think of difference is essential to the success of all students. Unless we do so, the negative messages that accompany deficit thinking will dominate, regardless of how well intentioned we may be or how highly recommended the instructional program we have adopted.

Racism in the 21st Century

Our assumptions about race and racism must also be deconstructed in that they, too, perpetuate the inequitable outcomes of schooling. Although I asserted above that, even in the first half of the 21st century, we fail to adequately discuss the way race plays out negatively and inappropriately in our society; nevertheless, many would argue that we are rarely free from the barrage of news about racial violence and accusations of racism in our media. Some might even assert, especially with the rise of Black Lives Matter, that race is too prominent in our thinking. To be sure, the issue is front and center of many articles and broadcasts; yet, I

am arguing here that disparities related to race are still too little understood and less well addressed in meaningful ways. Moreover, in American society race issues are often thought to be restricted to those who are Black or of African American heritage, neglecting other historic and present instances of racism against those who are Indigenous, Latino, Middle Eastern, or multi-ethnic. We think of ourselves as a society of opportunity, failing to acknowledge the barriers that have existed for so many and for so long. For example, miscegenation laws were only finally repealed in the United States in 1967 when the Supreme Court, in a decision known as *Loving v. Virginia*, found the prohibition to be unconstitutional.

Misegenation refers to marriage or cohabitation between two people from different racial groups.

It takes only a cursory examination of some data to recognize the continued inequities in education related to race. Black children represent 18% of pre-schoolers but 48% of pre-school children receiving more than one out-of-school suspension (CRDC, 2014); they are suspended at three times the rate of White students. (Yes, pre-schoolers really are being expelled in schools across the nation; Wynne [2015] calls them "virtual toddlers" [p. 365]). Latino and Native American students were 42% and 66% more likely than White peers to receive out-of-school suspensions (Advancement Project, 2010). Black students also represent 16% of total school enrollments but 27% of students referred to law enforcement and 31% of students receiving a school-related arrest. "The U.S. Department of Education reports that 81% of the class of 2013 graduated within four years," but that the graduation rate for American Indians is 70% and Blacks and Hispanics "continue to graduate at lower rates than Asians and whites" (Yettick & Lloyd, 2015). Sweeten (2006) found that a first-time arrest during high school nearly doubles the odds of a student dropping out, and a court appearance nearly quadruples those odds.

Here, one might also think of the reports of commissions investigating the early public schooling

and treatment of Indigenous populations in several countries: the stolen Aboriginal generation of Australia, the Canadian Truth and Reconciliation Commission on Residential Schooling, or the American attempts at assimilation of its American Indian populations. In Australia, in 2008, Prime Minister Kevin Rudd apologized to the Aboriginal population in an attempt to begin a process of healing that would ultimately eliminate disparities in living conditions in that country. In Canada, during the summer of 2015, a multi-year report on the status of Indigenous people released by the Canadian Truth and Reconciliation Commission found that the policy of governmental and church-run schools, in the name of offering education, was, in fact, a policy of cultural genocide (Austen, 2015). An apology has also been given for this process of forcing Aboriginal children from their homes, requiring them to give up their culture and language; this policy has recently been termed "cultural genocide."

As in the other two countries, in the United States, boarding school policies aimed at the elimination of Indigenous dress, language, and culture have resulted in longstanding depression, trauma, and disparities in living conditions for American Indians. Indigenous children confined to residential schools experienced a loss of their culture and language, being forced to cut off their hair, change their names, and being punished if they spoke their own language. Here, despite these and other policies aimed at the assimilation of American Indians and the elimination of their culture and languages, no formal apologies have been made.

Yet often an apology is inadequate. Acknowledgement without action is never transformative. Speaking of the Canadian report, King wrote (cynically, some would say):

> Here's what's most likely to happen. Those recommendations that are, in large part, cosmetic or symbolic may well be adopted. Any recommendations

with price tags attached—funding for improved health care on reserves—or recommendations that might open the government to legal action will be ignored. (2015)

It is to be hoped that King is wrong; yet, educators have long been cognizant of inequities related to race and ethnicity, with little substantive change occurring in most schools. Unfortunately similar situations exist almost universally as in Mexico, Australia, and New Zealand, among other countries, where Indigenous children have also been marginalized and vigorous attempts made to assimilate them. Few understand how being torn from family at a young age, forced to give up all ties to one's heritage, and to speak a "foreign" language may have led to uncertainty about one's own identity, one's ability to parent, or to live a productive and happy life.

Similarly, in the U.S., educators and citizens in general are rarely cognizant of the impact of raids conducted by Immigration and Customs agents on Spanish-speaking immigrant families and on the ability of their children and youth to complete their schooling. When agents wait outside of schools, arresting parents as they drop off their children, or when children arrive home after school, only to find their parents no longer there, it is little wonder that educational attainment is affected. Instead of responding with anger and blame, educators need to keep in mind the fact that children have absolutely no say in the situation. Remember, for example, the reasons for Gabriel's family's entry into this country and the subsequent contributions he has made; hence, we must respond with great compassion and empathy.

Recent news reports about police shootings of Black youth have brought to the public's attention disparities in arrest and conviction rates based on race and ethnicity, with such phrases as "Driving While Black" or "Black Lives Matter" becoming widespread. The historic Emmanuel AME Church

in Charleston, South Carolina, reopened its doors for worship soon after a 21-year-old White man shot and killed nine people, including the pastor. The shooter is purported to have done so, saying, "I have to do it ... You rape our women and you're taking over our country" (Ford & Chandler, 2015). Questions need to be asked: Where are the facts? To whom is he addressing his comments? Whose country is "our country?" How do people who have been here legitimately for centuries "take over" a country when they are under-represented in every position of power?

Where do his beliefs and similar White supremacist expressions come from? Why, in the wake of President Obama's 2008 election, hailed by some as proof we live in a "post-racial society," does racism still persist? Black people represent only 12% of the total population in the United States; the Hispanic population has increased to 17%. However, as Blacks and Hispanics are taking more prominent places in public life, acquiring professional positions and being elected to formal office, they have become more visible. Yet, proportionately, they still fall far short of their overall percent. So, how and why do people have the sense "they" are taking over? Overt racists like the Charleston shooter must have learned it somewhere, likely from friends and family, perhaps even at school, but also from elements in the wider culture. At the same time, statistics simply represent the tip of the iceberg—measurable incidents of racism that can be specifically identified in our society. They fail to acknowledge the deeply rooted "civilizational racism" (Scheurich & Young, 1997) that comprises the totality of our deepest assumptions about what constitutes "the real, the true, and the good" (p. 38). Yet this civilizational racism drives much of what still occurs and is taught in schools as well as in the wider society.

One further indication of how entrenched racism is in our society was provided by a study conducted in 2003 at the University of Chicago in which

researchers mailed thousands of identical résumés to employers with job openings and recorded which ones were selected for interviews. But before sending them, they randomly assigned stereotypically African American names (such as "Jamal") to some and stereotypically White names (like "Brendan") to others. The same résumé was roughly 50% more likely to result in a callback with the White name— despite the employers saying they prized diversity (Bertrand & Mullainathan, 2004).

Unfortunately, racism is alive and well in our society. If all people are to have equal opportunities for liberty and to pursue happiness, schools will need to play a central role in eradicating negative and disrespectful assumptions instead of turning a blind eye or assuming there is no further work to be done. In many schools and classrooms, race may be the foremost issue that needs to be addressed, with numerous assumptions needing to be deconstructed and then reconstructed in more equitable ways. But it is not the only mental model that must be challenged.

Sexual Orientation and Gender Identity

We also need to challenge the ways in which we think about sexual orientation and gender identity. Too many people still experience discrimination and marginalization for being lesbian, gay, bi-sexual, trans-gendered, or questioning (LGBTQ). In the 21st century, in our wider society, attitudes and beliefs are changing. In the United States, the June 2015 decision of the Supreme Court legalized same-sex marriage nationwide, overruling the laws of 14 states that had previously refused to do so. Partners of gay men and women are now permitted to receive many federal benefits—pensions, military healthcare benefits, and so forth; yet some benefits are still restricted to non-same sex married couples. At the same time as the Supreme Court ruling offered hope, a number of states passed new laws discriminating against gay people. Michigan,

for example, passed in June 2015, a law supporting the right of private adoption agencies—even though they receive state taxpayer support—to refuse to place children with gay adults. Twenty states have also passed versions of "religious protection laws." Originally prompted by the firing of two members of the Native American Church for taking part in a peyote ceremony, they are now being used to endorse and legitimize discrimination against "women, gays and lesbians or other groups" (Eckholm, 2015). Hence, religious protection laws no longer offer protection for minorities against discrimination.

In schools, discrimination based on sexual orientation persists as well. Stories of gay students being denied permission to bring a boyfriend or girlfriend to a school prom occasionally appear in the media; as did the recent account of Evan Young, a Colorado student with a 4.5 grade point average who wanted to use his valedictory speech to help create a more inclusive school environment by urging honesty on the part of everyone (and hence, by "coming out" himself). In his case, after much publicity about the school's refusal to let him give his speech, he presented it to a public fund-raising rally for gay rights, to the praise of several politicians and the delight of the crowd.

In many schools, children with gay parents suffer tremendously from these and other forms of legitimized discrimination. By June 2015, 18 states still failed to include being gay as an enumerated category of students who may be bullied; thus, ignoring the fact that "queer kids are 3 to 4 times more likely to be bullied because of their real or perceived sexual orientation or gender identity/expression than other kids due to issues of race, ethnicity, or disability" (Kosciw, Greytak, Palmer, & Boesen, 2014). In addition, students report that teachers interrupt or intervene in discriminatory speech situations less than 20% of the time. LGBTQ students exhibit poorer school performance, more absenteeism, higher rates of dropping out of

school, increased rates of drug abuse, risky sexual behaviors, depression, and anxiety, and are six times more likely to commit suicide than their heterosexual peers. There is a strong correlation between feeling accepted and school success.

In a public school, each taxpayer and his or her children have an equal right to respect, participation, and inclusion. How long will it take us to normalize the lived experiences of those who may be, in some ways, unlike us? Regardless of what we may have been taught by our families or our religious organizations, in public schools no students should be made to feel shame because of their sexual orientation or that of a family member. No students should have to go through the day so worried that someone will find them out that they cannot concentrate on the lesson. Gay students should not feel pressured to join in the taunting to hide their true selves or to find it necessary to invite someone of the opposite sex on a date to dispel rumors about who they really are.

One purpose of schooling is to help all students to develop to their fullest potential and, some would say, to contribute fully to a peaceable, sustainable, and prosperous society. This cannot happen if we do not fully accept and respect each person. Hence, transformative leaders must challenge any speech and any behavior that discriminates against students on the basis of sexual orientation or gender identity.

Social Class, Poverty, and Well-being

Another aspect of students' identity and lived experience comes from their family's social class and economic well-being. Although social class is generally thought to be a reflection of family income, parental levels of education, and employment status, we most often focus entirely on economic poverty. Sixteen million children in the United States live below the poverty line (set in 2013 at $23,624 for a family of four). As with other

social markers, all researchers agree that poverty does not affect all groups equally, although different sources report different percentages for subgroups. The U.S. Bureau of Statistics reported in 2013 that 39% of African American children, 35% of American Indian children, and 33% of Latino children live in poverty, while only 14% of White children (non-Hispanic) live in similar circumstances (*KIDS COUNT*, 2015).

In America, somewhere around 3 million people also experience homelessness on a given night, with one-third of them being children. Moreover, the group of unaccompanied homeless youth over 16 includes as many as 40% who self-identify as gay or transgendered. Homelessness is, of course, a dire form of poverty and requires particularly sensitive treatment on the part of teachers. These distinctions will be addressed later when I examine some ways to make our schools more inclusive and socially just, but for now, consider that the homeless comprise part of the group being described as children living in poverty.

We also know that families of children who live in poverty have less health insurance and, hence, poorer physical and mental health, less parental education, and less stable housing situations than those who are not as impoverished. In education, children who live in poverty have higher rates of absenteeism, increased chances of being suspended or expelled, and experience less school success than their more advantaged peers. In fact, children who live in poverty are seven times more likely to drop out of school than children from families with higher incomes (*KIDS COUNT*, 2015). Gabriel, living in a one-room apartment with four siblings and his parents, had much more to worry about than his homework; yet he was one of the lucky ones in that, despite their poverty, his parents emphasized educational success—even to the point of working several jobs each.

Although the above statistics are all accurate, they do not differentiate between children who

come from generational poverty and those experiencing situational poverty; each has its own characteristics that must be understood and addressed by transformative educators. Children who come from generational poverty (whose parents and/or grandparents have also experienced deprivation) are more likely to have limited experiences and knowledge of the wider world, lower vocabulary, less preparation for school, fewer books in the home, and so on. Children like Gabriel who live in situational poverty (a situation caused by illness, parental loss of a job, death of a parent, bankruptcy, civil unrest, etc.) are experiencing loss and trauma, but may still have benefitted from parents with education and more general knowledge. Both groups are likely to be hungry and to show evidence of being nervous, worried, and even ashamed of their situations although the causes and details will be very different.

It is important to continually remind ourselves that children do not choose to be poor or to be hungry. They do not choose to be ill or to move constantly from house to house. They do not choose their parents' circumstances. Nevertheless, they suffer the stigma of disrespect, discrimination, and often of being dismissed or disregarded as having little potential and less to offer. In turn, lack of school acceptance for their circumstances negatively affects their academic performance. Transformative educators must challenge any attitudes that imply that poor children cannot experience high academic achievement or attain lofty educational goals.

Language and Ethnicity

As of 2010, approximately 40 million people (13% of the U.S. population) were born outside of the country. Moreover, English Language Learners (ELL), students whose home language is not English or that differs from that of instruction in school, comprise approximately 20% of the public

school population. Unfortunately, for the most part, these students experience less school success than their (often) monolingual peers, despite having equal ability. In part, this is because the quest for appropriate ways to educate the one-fifth of public school children who were not born in United States is fraught with political overtones and notions of cultural hegemony.

The first formal attempt in education to introduce legislation to address the needs of non-English speaking children may be traced to the Bilingual Education Act of 1968. Since then little has changed except the number of ELL students needing to be better served. Gabriel's situation was a case in point. His story attests to numerous truths about English Language Learners and our school system. His parents worked night and day to support their five children, rarely having the ability to take (unpaid) time off work to appear at the children's school. Yet they cared desperately, having given up their own economic comforts to ensure the welfare of their children. They were well educated and understood the value of education, but their circumstances did not permit extensive involvement with homework. Additionally, having seven people living in a one-bedroom apartment meant that the children had few opportunities for quiet study.

Gabriel became a product of the deficit-thinking mindset applied to him by an educational system that failed to appreciate his lived experience and, as a result, had come to believe that he was "dumb" and that his future was limited. He internalized the incessant barrage of negative messages and repeated them constantly and resolutely to explain why he wanted to quit school. Although teachers often asked him for assistance with their own computer problems, none seemed to recognize that his ability with computers indicated untapped intelligence and unrecognized capacity. None advocated for him or even encouraged him to stay in school or to think about a future career.

Unfortunately Gabriel's story is not an isolated one. I personally know several other immigrant or English Language Learner students who were also misplaced in special education classes and left to languish, despite considerable intelligence; and I believe most educators would have the same knowledge. In every case, it took an advocate to recognize their ability and to encourage them, insisting that they be moved to "regular" classes where they could begin to fulfill their potential. In every case that advocate was not a teacher or principal. Indeed, educators were often the most insistent that because their English fluency was still developing they could not be expected to do more than manual labor. In one case, a teacher told a student who had come from Jamaica (speaking island English) that she should consider being a hairdresser, a waitress, or a house cleaner. She now holds a PhD and is an assistant superintendent in a large school district.

We misplace students, leave them to languish with low expectations, forbid them from making sense of instruction in their home language, and ultimately facilitate their dropping out of school, all because we do not understand their lived experiences and, instead, make unwarranted assumptions. This must stop. Every child deserves to have all educators believe in them, recognize and encourage their potential, and advocate for them. Until transformative educators take on this task, too many children, like Gabriel, suffer lost opportunity and diminished hope. And too many will therefore be lost to our democratic civil society.

Separation of Church and State in a "Christian Country"

One final area I want to explore briefly here is that of religious differences. Despite the assertion that this is a country of opportunity for everyone, where the establishment clause of the First Amendment ensures there is to be no state religion required or encouraged, that no particular religion

may be favored in law, and that religious adherence may not be favored or disfavored over non-adherence, our history of religious tolerance is not attractive. The early Puritan settlers, for example, demonstrated considerable intolerance and attempted to pass laws that kept both Quakers and Jews from inhabiting their new territory. In fact, historians tell us:

> The Puritans believed they were doing God's work. Hence, there was little room for compromise. Harsh punishment was inflicted on those who were seen as straying from God's work. There were cases when individuals of differing faiths were hanged in Boston Common. ("Puritan Life", n.d.)

Despite the fact that the United States of America was founded on the notion of religious freedom and offered a haven for those suffering religious persecution in their home countries, the first European settlers quickly saw others as non-desirable and practiced religious discrimination. Native Americans, for example, were considered to be inhuman savages who needed to be civilized or Christianized. Subsequently, to avoid discrimination, Jewish immigrants, who generally came to North America to escape anti-Semitism in Europe, quickly attempted to integrate into the existing culture, suppressing their language and establishing themselves as merchants. Nevertheless, they, too, experienced persecution and still, in some cases, believe they are not fully accepted today. Fine (1997) wrote in an article about housing discrimination published in the *Michigan Historical Review*:

> Blacks were not the only victims of housing discrimination; Jews and members of various ethnic groups were similarly affected. A 1958 survey of real-estate agents in the Detroit suburbs revealed that 56 percent of them discriminated against Jews in "varying degrees." As the nation learned in

1960, ... the affluent Grosse Pointe suburbs of Detroit had, since 1945, been using a screening system that discriminated against blacks, Jews, and other ethnic groups seeking to purchase homes there. (p. 84)

Today, the United States is not only a mosaic of ethnic groups but also of religious practices, with the four largest religious groups being Christianity, Judaism, Buddhism, and Islam. Although incidents of anti-Semitism still occur, with the rise of Islamophobia, it is fair to say that the most feared and misunderstood religious group in the United States in this century is Muslims. A case in point was the extensively reported pulling, in 2011, by Lowe's Home Improvement stores of an ad sponsoring the TV show "*All-American Muslim*" because of complaints by a group called the Florida Family Association. The basis for the complaint, apparently, was that the show displayed the families as "too normal" and failed to adequately present what they saw as the Islamic agenda's "danger to American values." This, of course, ignores the two centuries of Muslims living peaceably in this country and also negates the purported American values of tolerance, respect, and the right to religious freedom, again suggesting attitudes that must be confronted and reconstructed.

Since America's recent involvement in wars in the Middle East, beginning with the Gulf war in 1990, Americans have become increasingly aware of the prominent role played by Islam in many parts of the world. Most frequently, however, since the attack of 9/11, Islam has been incorrectly equated with terrorism and radicalism. We ignore the many contributions we take for granted on a daily basis that originally came from the Arabic world— contributions to our language, the arts, and to math and science. Our fear of Islamic terrorism leads to persecution of Muslim and Arabic students in our schools who are repeatedly subjected to taunts of "suicide bomber" and "'terrorist." Too often,

educators, believing teasing is a harmless teenage activity, also ignore these derisive comments.

Yet, the increased presence of Muslim students in our schools does pose challenges for educators. How do we provide appropriate accommodations so that public schools do not seem to marginalize Muslim students, while at the same time adhering to the intent of the establishment clause of the First Amendment? For some, offering a space for student prayer and reflection is anathema; for others it is a simple gesture to any student wanting a quiet place of retreat and reflection. How does one interpret New York City's decision to add two Muslim holy days to the two Jewish and two Christian holidays already recognized in the school calendar? Does this constitute undue attention and support of a particular religion or is it simply a gesture of respect to an increasingly large proportion of the student population? These and questions relating to curriculum, dress codes for physical education, and washroom and shower policy are presented when a transformative leader wrestles with the best ways to challenge persistent beliefs that religion and schooling must be kept separate.

In many ways, this "separation" interpretation of the First Amendment must itself be challenged, given that the clause simply asserts that there shall be no official state religion endorsed or practiced in public institutions, not that no religious practices are to be permitted. It is a fine line to be sure, but the real question for the transformative leader is how to create a safe, inclusive, and socially-just learning environment for everyone.

Other Belief Systems

The foregoing discussion does not preclude the need to deconstruct other belief systems as well, but is suggestive of some of the topics that transformative leaders must examine critically and reflectively if schools are to be transformed. There are

many others. How do we think of students with physical or mental challenges? How do we reject the stigma of mental illness? How do we address the teasing of those who may be "too heavy" or "too thin" and who decides what the norm is? Do we remain silent in our schools and classrooms when we know we have a student with a terminal illness in our classrooms, or when a student has experienced the sudden death of a friend or a family member?

Each time we remain silent, pushing an uncomfortable situation underground, we fail to help students grapple with difficult situations. And we fail to ensure that our schools are inclusive, enjoyable, and socially-just places of learning. Moreover, we send the message that people experiencing these situations are somehow not "normal." We must learn to address uncomfortable situations, and in so doing, to make our schools more accepting and inclusive of diverse perspectives and backgrounds.

All of the above relate to the second tenet of transformative leadership: belief systems that perpetuate inequity must be deconstructed if our public schools are to serve all students equitably.

What Do Reconstructed Frameworks Look Like?

To conclude this chapter, I want to begin to address a question to be taken up much more completely in chapters 4 and 5: What would reconstructed frameworks look like? How would schools be different if transformative leaders began to address issues of race, gender identity, religious belief, social class, poverty, and so on? And what difference would this make to all students?

First, the leader's decision-making lens will change. Instead of asking how a particular decision might improve test scores, or enhance the school's standing in the district, leaders will use the lens of equity and transformation as a basis for dialogue

and possible change. They will learn to ask, at every turn, questions such as:

- Who is marginalized and who privileged?
- Who is advantaged or disadvantaged?
- Who is included or excluded?
- Whose voices have been heard and who has held the power?

Second, as educators reject deficit thinking, transformative leaders will acknowledge that every child comes to school with capabilities (Nussbaum, 2006; Sen, 1992). Nussbaum (2006), for example, asserts that "many different types of lives have dignity and are worthy of respect." Although this should be a given, we sometimes ignore the dignity and worth of lives that are very different from our own. We forget that children like Gabriel who are English Language Learners already speak at least one language fluently; we ignore the ability of children from poverty to simply survive, sometimes preparing their own meals, changing a diaper for a younger sibling, or navigating alone a difficult public transit system. They may not speak correct formal English or know how the state legislature works, but they have lived experiences and perspectives that can form the basis for their learning, if we acknowledge and respect them.

Pedagogy is a comprehensive term that includes underlying ideology, the formal, informal, and hidden curriculum, and the strategies used to impart it to others.

Third, the pedagogical focus will change. Instead of trying to "cover the curriculum" or to ensure that students are prepared for test taking, the curriculum will build on students' lived experiences, helping each one to see his or her reality reflected in it. Weiner (2003) argues:

> Teachers as transformative leaders need to insert an ethical as well as a political discourse back into the language of education, confront the discourse of reactionary ideologues, and make visible to students and others alternative viewpoints as well as the mechanisms of power and domination that structure the corporate government complex

and the dismantling of democratic institutions. (pp. 101–102)

In other words, the curriculum will be broadened rather than narrowed to permit students to make sense of their world and to understand their place in it.

Finally, when every child sees himself or herself reflected in the curriculum, when all students can fully engage in the learning experiences without worrying about whether or not they belong in the school, more learning occurs. Disruptions for disciplinary incidents are reduced and test scores increase. Although transforming schools to be more equitable, inclusive, and socially just is simply the morally right thing to do, it is also a way—indeed the only way I know—to ensure that some of the proximal goals of schooling, including passing tests and obtaining a credential are attained.

Moving Forward

A 2010 UNESCO report, titled *Education Counts*, states,

> The equation is simple: education is the most basic insurance against poverty. Education represents opportunity. At all ages, it empowers people with the knowledge, skills and confidence they need to shape a better future.

To guarantee this insurance comes into force, we need transformation in our schools, beginning with beliefs, values, and assumptions that perpetuate inequities. Unless we start by deconstructing mindsets that perpetuate fear, distrust, and second-class citizenship, no new program or policy can succeed. New knowledge frameworks must be constructed in order for any change to be transformative and sustainable.

Now that we have begun to address beliefs and assumptions, in chapter three we examine the next two tenets of transformative leadership, tenets that demonstrate the importance of dismantling hegemonic power and distributing it appropriately both in schools and in the entire education system. There we will also explore the need for a balance between the individualistic and the collective goals (the private and the public good) of schooling and the consequences of an overemphasis on neoliberal and entrepreneurial goals.

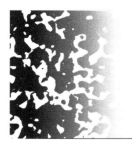

CHAPTER THREE

Power and Community

Sophie grew up in generational poverty with two parents who were on welfare. She recalls the stigma of being poor, saying she could feel the discrimination when she went to school. On "Welfare Wednesdays," when her parents had to take her with them to pick up their check because they could not be at the office and back before school was out, she heard people whispering about how inappropriate it was for her to miss school. Indeed, she says she was the "little girl people forgot at the back of the class."

As time went on, for various reasons, Sophie fell farther and farther behind academically. She did not learn to read. She was told she was too dumb to ever succeed in math. In fact, one year, when she was in high school, due to a temporary family situation, her parents pulled her out of school. The following year, when she re-enrolled in that same school, she found herself in the same math class, with the same teacher with whom she had struggled the previous year. So, her father summoned up his courage, overcame his own

fear of school, and went to see the principal. When he asked for Sophie to be put in a different math class, he was informed, "Your daughter is too stupid to succeed anyway, so it doesn't matter who her teacher is. All we can do is babysit her." Sadly, and with no knowledge of how the school worked or where to go next, he left the office, and soon, unsurprisingly, Sophie dropped out of school.

Fortunately Sophie's story does not end there. Years later, after a marriage breakdown and a divorce, alone, illiterate, and with two daughters to support, Sophie gathered her courage and enrolled in night school, determined not to be the parent who could not read to her children or understand the communications sent from their school.

* * *

In 1999, the Michigan state legislature removed Detroit's elected school board and replaced it with an emergency manager, amid allegations of corruption and mismanagement. Sixteen years later, and still considered a failing public school system, Detroit is under the watch of its fourth emergency manager. Its public school population has dropped from approximately 179,000 in 2000, to less than 50,000 in 2015, with 50,000 more students in charter schools, and another 6,500 in the 15 schools under the direct authority of the expensive and unsuccessful Education Achievement Authority that reports directly to the governor, bypassing all democratic processes. The fiscal surplus of 1999 has become a $250 million debt. In 2010, Michael Casserly, executive director of the Council on Great City Schools, commented on Detroit Public School's test results saying: "There is no jurisdiction of any kind, at any level, at any time in the 30-year history of NAEP that has ever registered such low numbers." He went on to cite the emergency manager who admitted that results were "barely above what one would expect simply by chance, as if the kids simply guessed at the answers" ("Detroit Public School Statistics," 2010).

With almost 20% of the current students assigned to special education classes, and a reported graduation rate in 2007 of less than 25% of beginning freshmen, Bob Wise, president of the Alliance for Excellent Education, discussed the impact on the state's economy, saying that a "high school dropout will probably be a tax consumer instead of a taxpayer and is much more likely to be incarcerated. Dropouts also earn about $260,000 less over their lifetime than those who complete high school" (Headlee, 2007).

In the first chapter, we examined the need for yet another leadership theory, finding that despite the myriad of current theories few, if any, focus in a comprehensive way on leadership that promotes equitable, inclusive, and socially just educational organizations. I also argued that transformative leadership is a way of life that holds the potential for such a change. In response, I identified eight distinct and discrete tenets of *transformative leadership* that are most successful and meaningful when taken together. Changing attitudes without changing actions benefits no one. Making the decision to change practices and policies is empty unless we consider the underlying assumptions and the goals of such changes and, hence, create more equity and justice.

The second chapter demonstrated that the starting point for transformation must be ourselves— our beliefs, values, and assumptions. We must then go on to help others with whom we work to examine their own frameworks and ultimately to dismantle and reconstruct those that perpetuate inequity. Once we have adopted new conceptual frameworks we can move to transforming the norms and operating procedures of the organization. New ways of acting as well as thinking must pervade every educational organization to overcome the Procrustean approach of modifying the traveller instead of the bed.

The two stories that begin this chapter are simply the tip of the iceberg in terms of the inequities and

injustices that occur on a daily basis in schools and school districts across the country. These and other similar ridiculous situations cry out for significant and sustained transformation. In this chapter, we shall explore the next two tenets of transformative leadership and examine how Tenet 3, **redistribute inequitable forms of power**, and Tenet 4, **establish a balanced emphasis on both private and public (individual and collective) good**, offer some additional ways of thinking comprehensively about changes that need to occur.

Who Holds the Power?

The foregoing discussion of mindsets that continue to privilege some at the expense of others has so far not addressed the issue of power. Yet it is because certain privileged groups have traditionally held the power, made the rules, and determined who may participate and who may not and on what terms—that we have a stratified society made up of an "in" group and those on the outside, sometimes known as those who experience "social exclusion."

Sophie's father did not hold power because he was on welfare and was consequently shown little consideration or respect by school personnel who certainly believed they "knew best" Sophie's abilities and potential. He had little education, was illiterate himself, and, thus, had really no way to influence the system.

On a systemic level, parents and taxpayers in Detroit also have little power (some would argue, because of Detroit's demographics); 83% of the population of Detroit is Black, about 7% Latino, 40% of the population lives below the poverty line, 50% of adults are either unemployed or looking for work, and, by some accounts, 47% of Detroit adults are functionally illiterate. This adds up to a population that lacks relative power in the state legislature, in part because the rest of the state's

demographics are reversed, with 80% of the overall state's population and the large majority of the legislature being White.

Although discrimination is difficult to prove, many indications suggest that race does play into the decisions of the legislature in Michigan and elsewhere throughout the United States. For example, Hana Brown summarizes previous research findings that "the higher the proportion of African Americans receiving cash welfare benefits, the more likely states are to adopt restrictive welfare policies." She goes on to report her subsequent analysis that "lawmakers used restrictive welfare changes as a strategy to appease white voters who felt threatened by other racial conflicts happening in the same period" (2015). A Washington State annual report asserts:

> Racially discriminatory lending practices have led to vastly inequitable outcomes for homeowners in the foreclosure crisis. African American and Latino borrowers were 30 percent more likely than whites to have been given a subprime mortgage, and this inequity exists across income brackets. For borrowers earning $150,000 to $250,000, the rate of subprime loans was 20 percent for whites, compared to 50 percent for Latinos and 62 percent for African Americans. As a devastating consequence, between 2007 and 2009, African American and Latino borrowers were 76 and 71 percent more likely than whites to lose their home to foreclosure. (Bocian, Li, & Ernst, 2010, p. 3)

And a 2007 report of racial justice and the American legal system found, "Minorities remain overrepresented in delinquency, offending, victimization, and at all stages of the criminal justice process from arrest to pretrial detention, sentencing (including capital punishment), and confinement" (Rosich, 2007, pp. 2–3).

Given the widespread acknowledgement of racial discrimination in American social structures,

it is beyond time that schools take the lead to engage in conversations and actions that would reduce such statistics. Discrimination is not simply a historical artifact but a present and living reality that results in marginalization and exclusion from full participation in our democratic society.

Exclusionary Practices

In 1849 Elizabeth Blackwell was the first woman to graduate from medical school in the United States; in 1905, Nora Stanton Blatch Barney was the first woman to graduate from Cornell in civil engineering. However, by 1960, only 1% of engineers in the United States were women. Moreover, examples of discrimination resulting in exclusion continue. Numerous private clubs still prevent women, people of color, or Jews from participating, although because enrollment standards are not necessarily a matter of public record, the exact number that discriminate on the basis of identity markers is unknown. What is known, for example, is that until the 1970s, when psychiatrist Dr. Leonard Ellison filed a lawsuit and became its first Black member, Black applicants were routinely rejected from the Detroit Yacht Club. The Augusta National Golf Club only permitted its first women members in 2012, and that same year it also became publically known that several clubs in New York also catered to an exclusively male membership.

In schools, reports of LGBTQ students excluded from school activities or children with Down syndrome or autism being suspended for disruptive activities are still too frequent. Sometimes the exclusion is dramatic as when, in 2009, a group of Black children attending a day camp at a private Philadelphia swim club were told to leave, because no minorities were allowed (Kilkenny, 2009). It was widely reported that when the Black children entered the pool, all the White children exited and one camper said, "I heard this lady, she was like, 'Uh, what are all these black kids doing here?'

She's like, 'I'm scared they might do something to my child.'" Subsequent reports indicated that although the day camp organization had previously paid its $1,900 membership fee, the day after the incident the organization received its check back in the mail without explanation. Other reports decried the comment attributed to the club's president, "There was concern that a lot of kids would change the complexion ... and the atmosphere of the club."

The Explanation: Power Inequities

The explanation for the swimming pool situation and all other instances of exclusion is simply power. Those who made the rules had enough power to exclude others, and those who were excluded did not have sufficient power to successfully resist. It is, thus, the presence or absence of power that results in curriculum decisions being made about what can and cannot be taught, about who is entitled to participate in formal presentations to children and who may not, and about whose voices are heard and whose are silenced.

Once again, some of the decisions made by powerful groups become well known, as in the Arizona decision to ban a controversial Mexican American history curriculum, even though it had been associated with increased graduation and achievement rates. Repeated attempts by conservative Christian groups to ban the teaching of evolution have been made in several states; and in June 2008, Governor Bobby Jindal of Louisiana signed a bill permitting teachers to use materials that challenged the ideas of both evolution and climate change. Other curricular revisions, such as those passed in Texas in 2010 and in 2015, have been widely reported, but what is not reported are the more subtle and persistent influences of those with power on both the formal and the informal curriculum, and on school policies and practices.

Almost universally, when discussions of the "achievement gap" between Caucasian and non-Caucasian children are reported, one of the reasons advanced is the limited participation of minoritized parents. The attendant solution is, of course, the encouragement of greater involvement by parents in their children's education, although the implication is always that parents need to come into the school at the organization's convenience, rather than being involved on their own terms and in their own way. This ignores, for example, the difference between a professional parent being able to take time off work (without losing pay) to attend a school function and the experience of many working-class people paid on an hourly wage basis, who may even live from paycheck to paycheck, and cannot afford to lose the wages required to attend their child's school activity during working hours.

Hegemony implies a form of non-violent domination that may be political, economic, or military. In the 20th century, Italian philosopher Antonio Gramsci used the term to imply social and cultural domination of the majority who impose their particular worldview on society as a whole.

Another problem with the belief that minoritized parents do not value or are not involved in their children's education is that this is generally an untruth. Most often, parents of families like Sophie's, who are not part of the mainstream power elite, do not feel comfortable in the school context. They may have had a negative experience with their own schooling; they may have been educated in a different culture and not feel knowledgeable about our school system; or they may believe that their legitimate role is to ensure children get to school on time, well fed and properly clothed, and that out of respect, it is appropriate to leave the decisions about formal education to educators. In any case, once again, a power imbalance may inhibit their participation, but this does not imply they place little importance on education.

Many critical educators and transformative leaders, however, have begun to reject the term *achievement gap* itself, arguing that once again, it places the responsibility on the child and family and ignores the social construction of schooling and the impact of hegemonic power on opportunities for minoritized students to fully participate or

succeed. Hence, the term *opportunity gap* has begun to replace that of achievement gap to signal that power and privilege come into play in students' school performance and that the education system bears some responsibility for the gap.

Moreover, when some people remain marginalized and outside of the decision-making structures of schools or society, their voices ignored or silenced, they are disempowered—denied the opportunity to exercise their democratic right to be heard and have their positions considered. This results in the more accurate concept of an empowerment gap[1] that must be taken seriously if transformation is to occur. This term *empowerment gap*, much more clearly than either achievement gap or opportunity gap, suggests that a power imbalance has been instrumental in maintaining a gap between those who traditionally perform well in schools and those who do not.

The power imbalance works in multiple ways to exclude parents from non-dominant groups whether religious, political, ethnic, economic, or cultural. We sometimes pat ourselves on the back when we have translated materials into various home languages represented in our schools. At the same time, we fail to recognize that this may be simply a necessary first step. If we invite parents who are unfamiliar with our schools to a parent-teacher conference, we can feel their anxiety level rise. What is the meeting for? What will they be expected to do? Who will talk? How should they dress? How long will it last? Who should attend? The questions are endless because they do not understand the "rules of power" governing the event.

The concept of power imbalance is also inherently present in the term *minoritized*, which I have used consistently to refer to populations about whom we need to challenge our assumptions. The

> Empowerment gap explicitly recognizes that gaps in test scores and student achievement are not necessarily, or even primarily, attributable to individual effort, but are strongly influenced by the inequitable and hegemonic power structures of public education.

> Minoritized refers to those groups who may or may not be in a numerical minority but who are in a subordinate position because of a power imbalance.

---

1 I was first introduced to this term by Dr. Gina Thésée, of the University of Quebec in Montreal (UQUAM).

term minoritized, as explained in Chapter 1, refers to those who may or may not be in a numerical minority but who are in a subordinate position because of a power imbalance. Hence, when schools on a Native Indian reservation with an almost 100% Indigenous student population celebrate American Indian week, the power imbalance and the incongruity of the situation are evident. How have their voices been so silenced that curricular decisions result in one special week being set aside for inclusion of Indigenous culture, instead of having their culture and heritage the basis for the whole curriculum? Similarly, in a place like Detroit, where the public school population comprises a roughly 91% Black (and 3% White) student population, how do Black history and culture remain largely excluded, except perhaps, during Black history month? Detroit's curriculum and standards are no different from those approved by the state for the neighboring Grosse Point school districts where the population makeup is reversed (9% Black and 89% White).

To some people the fact that all students experience a similar curriculum and take the same tests will seem normal. It is, after all, the situation with which we are all familiar and have experienced since the inception of our public schools. It is time to begin to ask ourselves, "Why?" Why is it right to have a curriculum that ignores, and actually misrepresents, the history of non-Caucasian settlers in this country? Why is it appropriate to perpetuate a Eurocentric curriculum with its limited perspective on "great books?" Why is it permissible for politicians to revise the list of reasons for slavery? These and other questions must be asked by transformative leaders who wish to create more inclusive and equitable schools.

Power Is Also Systemic

More broadly, when we examine the fight for inclusion and equal rights for all people in the United

States, two events likely come to mind: the passing of the Thirteenth Amendment in 1865, marking an official end to slavery, and the Nineteenth Amendment to the constitution in 1920, giving women the right to vote and to run for elected public office. However, it took another 35 years for Black women to overcome the requirements for literacy tests and other obstacles that still excluded them from the rights due to them. By 2015, almost 100 years later, women held only 104 (19.4%) of the 535 seats in the 114th Congress (33 of these were women of color); 20 more White women served in the Senate; and only six state governors were women.

The story of the decline of Detroit's public schools illustrates, however, that power imbalances do not only persist to exclude certain individuals on the basis of language, social class, or other individual identity markers; it also demonstrates that power imbalances are systemic. The imposition of four emergency managers by the state, the initial acquisition of Detroit Public Schools' fiscal surplus, and the subsequent refusal to assist with the huge debt incurred by the emergency managers—all point to actions taken, not only by individuals, but sanctioned throughout systems. Similarly, it is hegemonic power that perpetuates debates over how to interpret the history of Mexicans in America, that denies the scientific evidence of climate change, and that requires the inclusion of elements such as creationism into certain curricula.

It is power that continues to emphasize standardized tests that represent a middle-class European bias to the exclusion of many other kinds of knowledge. One common example is the Miller Analogies Test, often required for entry to graduate school. I recall enjoying my review for the test, in part because I happen to like puzzles and brainteasers, in part, because the questions took me back to places I had had the opportunity to visit—the Uffizi Gallery in Florence, the Prado in Madrid, the walled city of Cartagena in Colombia. By then,

however, I recognized, that the privilege of my life experiences gave me a tremendous advantage. Current web-based practice tests include questions such as: Cubism is to Picasso as (_?_) is to Dali. Others provide possible responses in parentheses such as (_?_) is to PUCCINI as SCULPTURE is to OPERA (Cellini, Rembrandt, Wagner, Petrarch); or MAUNA LOA is to ETNA as HAWAII is to (_?_) (Sicily, Alps, Crete, Bosporus).[2] These tests purport to measure thinking ability and one's capacity to identify logical relationships, but in reality they test experience and culture as well. To respond to a question about Cubism and Picasso and how it relates to Salvador Dali and Surrealism, one would not only need to have taken a class that teaches modern Western art but studied different movements—or had the opportunity to visit art galleries (perhaps even the Dali museum in St. Petersburg, Florida, which I happen to know because my parents lived nearby and had taken me to visit— another stroke of luck— and privilege).

The point is that we too often make assumptions about students' abilities based on test scores that privilege certain cultural and socio-economic groups and have absolutely nothing to do with inherent intelligence or ability. They continue to represent hegemonic power, to perpetuate our mental models of what knowledge is important and what is of lesser importance, and then to classify and categorize school success based on these notions.

Power operates in ways that affect the opportunities of individuals to participate fully in the experiences of schooling. It also functions to determine what counts as knowledge, as success, as achievement, and what is not valued or included in these concepts. It brings some groups of people into the mainstream of decision making and excludes others. In fact, the issue of power is so entrenched

---

2   For these and other questions see the practice tests provided at http://www.majortests.com/mat/miller-analogies-test-practice.php

and so all-encompassing that if we fail to acknowledge how pervasive it is, influencing all of the norms and practices of public schooling, including curriculum, pedagogy, testing, and many other policies and practices, then we will continue to support an empowerment gap. Transformative leaders will keep this issue at the forefront of decisions and of the ways in which they conceptualize the goals and purposes of education itself.

Goals and Purposes of Education

To some, it is a revelation that the goals and purposes of education are contested. In fact, I sometimes give workshop participants a list of possible goals of education and ask them to identify those that represent their top three priorities. Sometimes, they identify, as their priorities, statements such as:

- To help each student fully develop his or her intellectual abilities
- To teach students to be caring and empathic human beings
- To help students acquire the knowledge, skills, and understanding to be successful in a career.

Other members of the same group may select statements similar to the following:

- To ensure a prosperous and sustainable economy
- To prepare involved and knowledgeable citizens
- To increase the quality of life for our democratic society.

It then may come as a surprise for people to recognize that in some ways these statements represent

competing goals—the first three aiming at private or individual good and the second group focusing on more collective or public good outcomes. They are, of course, related in that it is important for individuals to be successful if we are to have a strong and sustainable democracy, but individual success alone does not ensure mutual benefit; hence the need for Tenet 4 and a **balanced emphasis on private and public good**.

Above, I suggested the need to redistribute power on both an individual and a collective level. This is, however, only one aspect of the need to balance both private and public good. Bob Wise's association of the failure of Detroit public schools with a loss of individual earnings on the part of Detroit students and their inability to pay taxes emphasizes the private good aspect of schooling. However, in the interview, he also emphasizes the subsequent burden on taxpayers. He reports, "If we could have just improved the graduation rate one half in Michigan, it would have meant $105 billion more coming in this year to the economy" (Headlee, 2007). Although economic goals must not be the only or even the primary ones considered, his statement does remind us of the public good of schooling. Education does contribute to the overall economy; moreover, it also contributes to the preparation of citizens who strive to make the country a better place for all.

Our current preoccupation with standardized test scores and college and career readiness has de-emphasized the civic goals and overemphasized the role of individual success and achievement. Yet, the transformative leader will recognize the importance of balancing the two. Helping each student to achieve his or her potential is obviously a critical function of education; however, as the story of Gabriel in the previous chapter illustrates, it is somehow not universally accepted. At the same time, putting Gabriel in front of a computer, where he could receive tutorials to improve his reading and/or math skills and, hence, better succeed in

passing the required tests, might have enhanced his argument to be put in a "regular" class; but it would not have helped him to make friends or to become a caring and responsible citizen, knowing and sometimes even questioning the values of his new society.

Private Good Goals

Private good is a term that focuses on benefits that accrue to an individual due to his or her own efforts.

There is no doubt that there have been some positive aspects to emphasizing private good. Encouraging students to persist in their education with the promise of increased lifetime earnings, better health and general welfare, and a more stable and comfortable future lifestyle is not a negligible outcome. A heartening fact in the second decade of the 21st century is that high school graduation rates have risen to an historic high of approximately 78%[3] (Stillwell & Sable, 2013). Moreover, a focus on preparing every child and disaggregating data to ensure that no sub-group's lack of attainment is masked in higher overall averages should result in the academic success of every child, the end to discriminatory and unequal treatment, an end to an excessive number of students being left to languish in special education or English Language Learner classrooms, and so forth. Nevertheless, there are also a number of negative consequences, which, at present seem to emerge from the disproportionate emphasis on the individual and neglect of the collective good.

Social mobility refers to the ability of individuals to change their economic and social status in life, that is, to move from a lower to a higher social class (or the reverse).

In Chapter 1, I cited David Labaree's (1997) notion that social mobility goals, which focus on preparing students to compete for positions that lead to individual attainment and success, have overshadowed goals relating to citizenship. Labaree argues that an undue focus on preparing students for workplace and career has resulted in education

---

3   Measured as those who graduate within four years of entering ninth grade (NCES, 2013).

being commodified and, hence, often privatized. It emphasizes what he calls "vocationalism" and the demands of a market-based economy rather than valuing a well-rounded education. Instead of leading the quest for a better society, education takes its lead from the demands of industrial profiteers who argue the need for education to provide future workers with specific skills rather than to develop the critical curiosity that may advance the well-being of everyone. The curriculum is narrowed and only what is tested is valued. Moreover, what is tested becomes what is taught, to the exclusion of many legitimate subjects (such as art, literature, and music).

This is not a new trend. Labaree cites the 1996 example of Michigan shifting "funds from adult education into job training, since, as the head of the state Jobs Commission put it, 'It's more important to align adult education programs with the needs of employers rather than to educate people for education's sake'" (Cole, 1996, in Labaree, p. 47). The focus on competition, both nationally and internationally, is seductive and, again, long-standing. Beginning with George Bush's goals identified in 1989 and reiterated by Clinton's *Goals 2000*, one explicit goal was that "United States students will be first in the world in mathematics and science achievement." Unfortunately, this leads, once again, to a narrowing of the curriculum, to an emphasis on competitive test scores, and to a reduction in the importance of dialogue leading to increased understanding of living together in mutual benefit.

What, in fact, does "best in the world" mean? Is it the most financially successful? The most innovative? Exhibiting the highest test scores? The most equitable? This notion of being "best" has somehow, in recent years, become associated with the concept of America being "exceptional," with a notion that "only in America" can certain things happen, or with the concept that America is the world leader in everything and must remain that

way. In fact, the concept of American exceptionalism was, originally, not simply a patriotic expression of national pride but a term used by De Toqueville in 1931 to assert of America:

> Their strictly Puritanical origin, their exclusively commercial habits, even the country they inhabit, which seems to divert their minds from the pursuit of science, literature, and the arts, the proximity of Europe, ... have singularly concurred to fix the mind of the American upon purely practical objects.

The paragraph continues, "Let us cease, then, to view all democratic nations under the example of the American people, and attempt to survey them at length with their own features." Subsequently, the term *American exceptionalism* was associated with the concept of Manifest Destiny, a belief in the superiority of the White settlers that permitted the acquisition, in the first half of the nineteenth century, of lands occupied by Native Americans or Mexicans. Historian Pfaff, as he critiques both concepts, writes, "It has become somewhat of a national heresy to suggest the U.S. does not have a unique moral status and role to play in the history of nations and therefore in the affairs of the contemporary world. In fact it does not" (2010).

Although American exceptionalism is typically used today as an expression of national pride, we must be cautious about assuming that everything American is superior to everything else. Indeed, another phrase so often thrown about casually, "only in America," is more indicative of lack of global awareness than of justifiable American pride.

The perpetuation of individualist and competitive goals has been associated by Giroux (2005) and others with the rise of neoliberalism and the perpetuation of inequity and disparities in our society. Because the market so often drives decisions, neoliberalism "wages an incessant attack on democracy, public goods, and non-commodified values" (Giroux, 2005, p. 2). Giroux goes on to say:

Neoliberalism refers to a belief that personal liberty is maximized by limiting government interference in the operation of free markets.

With its debased belief that profit-making is the essence of democracy, and its definition of citizenship as an energized plunge into consumerism, neo-liberalism eliminates government regulation of market forces, celebrates a ruthless competitive individualism, and places the commanding political, cultural, and economic institutions of society in the hands of powerful corporate interests, the privileged. (p. 8)

The result of this emphasis is the perpetuation, indeed perhaps the growth, of societal stratification and a lack of will or commitment to address inequality. Indeed, the more entrenched these forces become, the less inequality is considered an outcome of production, and the more individuals are blamed for being lazy, not trying hard enough, and so on—aspects we described in the last chapter as "deficit thinking" and as ideas that needed to be deconstructed.

As Labaree says, "The last thing a socially mobile educational consumer wants out of education is the kind of equal educational outcome produced in the name of democratic equality" (p. 51). In other words, those who are already successful may be content to ignore, or even to perpetuate, inequity in the name of preserving their own social or economic benefit. Good examples are the persistent desire for limited access to advanced placement courses, differential access (in some cases based on parental recommendations or contributions) to gifted programs or to Ivy League colleges with the best reputations. From this desire to minimize educational mobility, educational benefit becomes a zero sum game with winners and losers. And in many ways, this is exactly what the current test mania has produced.

Moreover, the undue emphasis on schools as a private good has resulted in what some see as the potential demise of public schooling. Labaree said it best almost a decade ago, and the trend has accelerated since then:

Charter schools and consumer choice are the current icons. The word *public* itself is being transformed, as public schools are renamed *government* schools (with all the stigma that is carried by this term in an anti-government era), and private charter schools are being christened *public school academies* (the title accorded them by law in Michigan). (p. 73)

Yet, the survival of a democratic society depends on everyone having a high quality education and having developed a strong sense of civic virtue.

Public Good Goals

We must reinstate the general acceptance of education as a public good evidenced, for example, by Thomas Jefferson, who argued for citizens not to have control of government removed from them, but to be enlightened through education in order to be fully able to exercise their constitutional power. He is recorded as saying in a letter to William C. Jarvis in 1820:

Public good refers to benefits that accrue to the population as a whole indirectly, e.g., an increase in the general level of education is associated with a decrease in incarceration costs.

I know no safe depositary of the ultimate powers of the society but the people themselves; and if we think them not enlightened enough to exercise their control with a wholesome discretion, the remedy is not to take it from them, but to inform their discretion by education. This is the true corrective of abuses of constitutional power. (Peterson, 1984)

Despite his firm belief in the power of education, his desire to institute free schools for all children in Virginia, and his founding of the University of Virginia, Jefferson's views remained somewhat elitist, believing education was for all "free children" who were, of course, White. Others, whose views have been more generalizable, have also argued the centrality of education to democratic

society; in other words, they have stressed the public good of education. Barber (2001) writes, "The fundamental task of education in a democracy is the apprenticeship of liberty—learning to be free" (p. 12). For him, this has long been the task of education:

> The meaning of *public* education was precisely education into what it meant to belong to a public: education in the *res publica*—in commonality, in community, in the common constitution that made plurality and difference possible. (p. 19)

Moreover, Barber not only believes that education is the cornerstone of democracy in that it is the way in which democratic citizens are formed; but he expresses his fundamental belief in, and respect for, all members of society when he argues that education must be available to everyone:

> For true democracy to flourish ... there must be citizens. Citizens are men and women educated for excellence—by which I mean the knowledge and competence to govern in common their own lives. The democratic faith is rooted in the belief that all humans are capable of such excellence and have not just the right but the capacity to become better citizens. (pp. 12–13)

Lauder takes the argument one step farther, positing that the "requirements of an education for democracy" are:

> High overall level of achievement so that students have the understandings and skills required to participate in a democratic society and an open, non-selective system of education which promotes equality of results. A strong notion of equality of opportunity of this kind is required because in a society differentiated by ethnicity, gender and class in which those who conceive policy are nearly always highly educated, a voice needs to be given to

those who do not traditionally succeed in education. (1991, p. 390)

Although I would likely have chosen the word *equity* instead of *equality of opportunity*, one can see here a strong argument for balancing the private good with clear understandings of the public good. Lauder's point is that in a society characterized by diversity, those who have power by virtue of being "highly educated" do not always necessarily listen to those who are less educated. The role of education, he argues, is to help everyone understand how to participate in a democratic society.

Transformative leadership takes this concept farther, arguing that students not only need to learn how to participate but also to understand how power actually works to marginalize some and privilege others, to silence some voices and to privilege others. Dewey was convinced that this kind of education occurred best when children from various backgrounds were brought together so "each such group exercises a formative influence on the active dispositions of its members." In fact, he saw education in the diverse setting of public schools as the only way in which

> the centrifugal forces set up by juxtaposition of different groups within one and the same political unit [can] be counteracted. The intermingling in the school of youth of different races, differing religions, and unlike customs creates for all a new and broader environment. (1916/2008, ch. 2)

Given the rapidly changing demographics of some schools and districts and the increase in visible diversity, this perspective becomes perhaps even more important in the 21st century than 100 years ago when Dewey first made that assertion. One role of public schools is to bring together children from the diverse groups in society and to help them create new understandings. Instead of circling the wagons and becoming entrenched in fear

and prejudice, this bringing together of those from different backgrounds creates, in Dewey's words, something new and broader.

One area illustrative of the importance of thinking about the balance between private and public good is that of education policy. Too often we think of policies in terms of individual behavior, but thinking differently may bring not only new understandings but improved practices as well. To illustrate, we will consider an important area of policy—that of school discipline, although the same considerations could also apply to policies related to attendance, extra-curricular activities, scheduling, and so forth.

Democratizing Discipline

In Chapter 1, we identified the presence of disproportionate disciplinary incidents among minoritized youth. A study by the Office of Civil Rights of the USDE found that although students with disabilities represent only 12% of students, they represent nearly 70% of the students who are physically restrained by adults in their schools (OCR, 2012). The study also found:

> In districts that reported expulsions under zero-tolerance policies, Hispanic and African American students represent **45 percent** of the student body, but **56 percent** of the students expelled under such policies. (emphasis in original)

An Individualistic (Private Good) Interpretation. At first glance, interpreted as a result of individual misbehaviour (i.e., of private good or lack thereof), these statistics may seem appropriate. The manifestation of certain types of disability may be behavioral issues and so it may seem reasonable that students exhibiting behavioral challenges require additional restraint. It may be irrefutable that certain students seem more angry and less engaged in school activities than others; hence the

interpretation that if African American or Hispanic or gay students act out more often, they should be punished for their inappropriate behavior. Similarly, if a school has a zero tolerance policy, it may make sense that those who swear, disregarding the policy, should suffer the consequences of their inappropriate language.

However, this is simply the tip of the iceberg. Individual behavior is not innate. Students do not misbehave because they are Black or Hispanic or gay. They are not born angry, or swearing, or bullying and so forth. Just as we have stated earlier that children do not choose to be homeless or to be poor, they also do not choose the culture into which they are born. Consider the differences among the lived experiences of Ricardo, Adrian, and George. Ricardo is the fourth of six children from a family that recently immigrated to the United States. His father is working (when possible) as a construction laborer; the mother works evenings as a waitress. Although they care deeply about each other, the family's normal interaction pattern involves a lot of yelling at one another, punctuated by a great deal of swearing (in almost every sentence). On the other hand, Adrian is the only child of a middle-class conservative, fundamentalist Christian family who attend church Wednesday and Sunday evenings as well as Sunday morning. Adrian's family never swears and he has never heard terms like "gay" or "faggot" at home. George, who is a thirteen-year-old boy from an atheistic, White, middle-class family, has recently been diagnosed with Tourette's syndrome, and exhibits both sudden verbal and non-verbal tics that his teacher claims frequently disturb the classroom learning environment.

If a school's discipline policy is rigid, listing punishments associated with specific behaviors, it is likely that Ricardo and George will be punished significantly more frequently than Adrian, even though they may be trying hard to behave. On the other hand, considering the specific circumstances

in George's case, which is likely accompanied by a note from a doctor attesting to his inability to control his behavior, will likely lead to consideration of the need for differential treatment.

But what about Ricardo? Here it may be useful to reflect on the purpose of the school's discipline policy. If it is simply to punish inappropriate behavior, Ricardo will likely find himself spending more and more time outside of the classroom and soon will fall behind academically, with the statistically likely outcome of eventually dropping out of school. If on the other hand, there is an educational purpose to the policy, the school will institute practices intended to help Ricardo to self-censor his language and to find more acceptable ways of expressing himself. This will take time. It is not easy to change patterns of thought or language and Ricardo goes home every day to hear language that, at school, he is told is not appropriate. If he slips from time to time, as he expresses himself in general conversation or interaction with peers, should the full force of the policy be implemented? If Ricardo and Adrian both are heard to swear at a teacher, whose words are more likely to be a deliberate contravention of policy? Again, there are multiple perspectives here. If Adrian swears at a teacher, he is obviously extremely upset and the reasons should certainly be investigated. Ricardo's expression may, on the other hand, reflect only a mild irritation to which he has responded reflexively.

> Discipline does not imply punishment but rather a form of instruction that helps the learner to self-regulate.

It is critically important for educators to reflect on the purposes of a discipline policy and, indeed, the meaning of the word *discipline* itself. Its roots are in the Latin word *disciplina*, which meant "instruction"—not originally punishment and yet, somehow, it has too often lost its original meaning. Dictionary definitions include "systematic training in obedience to regulations and authority" and "the state of improved behaviour, etc., resulting from such training or conditions." Discipline, as instruction toward desired behavior, should be an

integral component of a democratic education that transforms both understandings and behaviors.

One might wonder how we have come to adopt the punitive legalistic approach of some geopolitical entities and instituted zero tolerance policies in our schools. Skiba and Rausch (2006) emphasize,

> There is **little or no evidence** that strict zero tolerance policies have contributed to reducing student misbehavior or improving school safety. Studies of suspension have consistently documented that **at-risk students do not change their behavior as a result of suspension**; that suspension is associated with school dropout and juvenile incarceration; and that schools with higher rates of suspension and expulsion tend to have lower test scores and a less satisfactory school climate. (National Center on Inclusive Education, n.d., p. 2, emphasis in original)

Their assertion is important. Behavior does not normally change as a result of punishment. Educator Eric Jensen (2013) supports this point, asserting, "Praise, punishment, and extrinsic rewards are the least useful forms of feedback" (2013, loc. 1445).

Nevertheless, media reports are replete with examples of children who have been expelled or suspended because of behaviour found egregious under zero tolerance policies. The *St. Petersburg Times*, for example, reported that when a 10-year-old girl found a small knife in her lunchbox, placed there by her mother for cutting an apple, she immediately gave it to her teacher but was expelled from school for possessing a weapon. The *Atlanta Journal-Constitution* described how a teen in Columbus, Georgia, was expelled for violating school rules by talking to his mother (with whom he had not spoken in 30 days) on a cell phone while at school; his mother was on deployment as a soldier in Iraq. In yet another incident, an 11-year-old at a middle school in Highlands Ranch, Colorado, took a

lollipop from a jar on the teacher's desk and was charged with theft. The boy was convicted of a misdemeanor and put on probation.[4]

These are undoubtedly extreme examples, but the fact that they have occurred at all in our schools suggests that something is drastically wrong with the ways in which we conceive of discipline. Somehow we forget that we are dealing with vulnerable children, like Sophie and Gabriel, who are learning to conform to societal norms and expectations. We ignore developmentally appropriate responses and criminalize young students. Certainly, these policies focus on school safety by removing students from the educational setting but they do little to either change behavior or to foster learning and self-discipline on the part of the student. They do even less to remediate the social conditions that often exacerbate negative behavior. This inappropriate and excessive reaction is not, however, the only problem with current approaches to discipline.

A Collective (Public Good) Interpretation. To be sure, when students are not in school, they cannot disrupt the learning environment, but neither are they learning—either the prescribed curriculum or ways of living peacefully together in a democratic society. If one of the fundamental purposes of education is to teach citizenship, then keeping the peace by excluding students will not accomplish that broader goal.

Given the disproportionate levels of suspension, expulsion, restraint, and drop-out rates of minoritized students—that is, those who in some way are not typical of the White, middle-class norm—transformative educators must ask themselves why and how this occurs. Are African American students genetically predisposed to violence? Are Latino students genetically predisposed

4 These and other incidents were reported in Issue Brief No.1 published in 2014 by the U.S. Department of Education Office for Civil Rights.

to swearing? Are LGBT students genetically prone to lashing out when they are bullied? Or is something else going on?

This is where the notion of public or collective good becomes important. It is important to take into account the historic oppression and marginalization of certain groups and sub-groups in society. This includes disproportionate placement of African American and Latino male students in special education programs, disparate suspension and expulsion of LGBTQ students for retaliating for constant bullying, unequal placement of English Language Learners in lower-level vocational programs, denial of female Muslim students the right to wear the hijab or to cover arms and legs during physical education or swim lessons, and so forth.

I recall a series of frustrating conversations with a school principal whose population had recently changed from almost entirely Caucasian to one that included an increasingly large number of students who had recently emigrated from an African country. Many of these recent arrivals, he reported, were habitually engaged in inappropriate behavior at school, including fighting, and, hence, were regularly suspended or even expelled. When I asked what was going on, the principal's response was that these were the students who were fighting and, therefore, were the ones who needed to be punished according to the school discipline policy. When I asked why they were fighting, he indicated that they were simply angry, likely due to negative factors in their home situations, and sometimes due to being teased for their accents, and were taking out their frustrations at school.

This principal's position is not uncommon. We argue that it is unfortunate that our prisons are disproportionately filled with young Black men, but that they are the ones who have committed the crimes. We believe it is all right to engage in racial profiling of Middle Eastern men because, after all, they are the one who are terrorists, and so on. If LGBT students, tired of hearing slurs and being

teased, lash out against those who have consistently bullied them, we argue that they must learn to better control themselves. If children from economically disadvantaged families are absent from school to look after younger siblings while their parents cash welfare checks to buy food, or if youth from undocumented families are late to school, having fed breakfast to younger siblings and accompanied them, first, to their schools because their parents have been detained, the full force of school policies is frequently aimed at them without any thought being given to how our social and economic systems contribute to the inability of some groups to participate fully and equally in organizations like schools.

Instead of examining the culture of our schools and communities to uncover ways in which it continues to exclude, marginalize, and disadvantage some groups of students, well-meaning educators too often simply adopt strict discipline policies or well-meaning anti-bullying programs that focus on the modification of individual behavior, but leave the underlying causes unaddressed. To remedy this situation, transformative educational leaders must focus on the underlying issues, address institutional racism and systemic discrimination, and not simply focus on individual behavior. This was the issue I tried to help the school principal understand. How were the students who were fighting being treated in the school and in the wider society? Were they being given covert and implicit messages that they did not belong? Were they subject to taunts and teasing related to race, ethnicity, and gender identity? Was the fact that they had home and family responsibilities well beyond the norm being taken into consideration? The principal insisted that day after day these were the students who were fighting, that their behavior was unacceptable, and that they needed to be punished.

To be sure, fighting is not an acceptable response, but it is very unlikely to be the only behavior needing to be corrected. If the overall culture of the school is hostile or unwelcoming or perhaps even unsafe for a given group of students, how can we change the underlying culture and structures? If discipline policies are to be a part of the informal curriculum, helping all students to learn to be caring citizens, how can we ensure that they work to promote democracy rather than to further marginalize some groups by excessive separation and punishment? Discipline must not simply respond to individual behavior.

There are no prescriptive responses to these questions because the answers will come from each context as transformative educators examine the practices and policies of their own organizations; nevertheless, acknowledging the need to incorporate both the public and private good in areas such as curriculum and policy is an essential task of the transformative leader.

The Need for Balance

It becomes clear, therefore, that promoting both public and private good has long been a fundamental task of education. Individual attainment of knowledge, skills, and dispositions is essential for students to become contributing members of a prosperous and sustainable society. Yet, if the concepts "prosperous" and "sustainable" are emphasized over those of democratic and equitable, then the stratified and competitive nature of education will prevent the acquisition of understandings necessary for full participation in democratic life. In that case, power dimensions—what Dewey called "the centrifugal forces" of a diverse society—will pull the society apart, increasing hatred and suspicion and inhibiting the promise of liberty and equality for all.

For that reason, redistribution of power underlies the ability to enhance the public good of both education and society. Given the increasing

diversification of society, communities, and educational institutions, it is no longer appropriate for only middle-class, largely White groups of citizens and elected officials to make the rules—explicit and implicit—that govern who may be included and who excluded, or who may be heard and who silenced. Somehow, transformative educational leaders must open spaces for every member of the school community to participate respectfully and to be respected, to value one another and to be valued, in order for the desired individual and collective learning to occur.

In the next chapter we examine ways in which this may take place as we focus on transforming learning goals to be more centered on issues of emancipation, democracy, equity, and social justice, and to encompass awareness of our interconnectedness and interdependence with others in the global community.

Once transformative leaders have helped to develop critical consciousness throughout the school community, reconstructing mental models in more equitable ways, broadening the base of those who have power and influence, and ensuring the inclusion of all people and perspectives, we have a basis for truly transforming our schools and educational institutions.

Transforming Action

At night school, Sophie found a teacher who inspired and encouraged her, who made learning fun. The students laughed and learned together. Sophie progressed so well that one day her instructor suggested she should think about going on to university and becoming a teacher. Sophie was amazed. Was her teacher joking? How could she, a failure, a student too dim-witted and thickheaded to pass math, ever succeed at university and become a teacher?

But the instructor persisted, helping Sophie to understand that it was exactly her struggles, and her success, that would give her the understanding and empathy to become an outstanding teacher. And ultimately, Sophie, like Gabriel, began to deconstruct the messages she had been given throughout her schooling experiences, and to understand that she had internalized the same deficit messages she had been given repeatedly. She acquired her GED. She went on to university. And she is now a teacher! As she makes a

difference every day for her students, her constant plea is to "believe in all students."

***

*Test day is tomorrow. As the students arrive at school, they are greeted with smiles, high fives, and a few hugs by Principal John Law. Denise says excitedly, "This is our **Who Is Your Neighbor Day**, isn't it?" Katie chimes in, "I can hardly wait to Skype again with our partner class in India!" Robert adds, "I want to go back to that book, Wake Up World! I can hardly believe the picture that showed Kim in Vietnam with all his possessions; they would fit in my dresser drawer!"*

Surprisingly, the students in Quiet Waters Elementary School are not sitting silently at their desks learning test preparation strategies. Teachers are not desperately trying to review key concepts in math or science. Instead, they are discussing the schedule that will permit every child in the school to cycle through a number of creative activities, helping them to learn more about themselves as they interact with others. Even very traditional Mrs. Sharp, whose academic focus emphasizes test scores as measures of academic achievement, has agreed to participate.

Dr. Law reports that teachers and parents believe it is important to de-emphasize testing and to remove some of its stress and pressure, hence the scheduling of the day. During the year, the faculty had created a survey for students that included pictures of kids from all over the world. Depending on the grade level, students were asked, "Which of these kids is nice? Which will be a nurse? A farmer? An engineer?" He stated that, perhaps not surprisingly, the students' responses were predictably stereotypical, with female images being assigned roles like nursing, and male roles like farming—something else he wanted to address.

Then the whole school engaged in book studies to help them learn about others, not in a paternalistic, missionary way, but to understand the complexity and diversity of the world. For example, to attempt to

counteract stereotypes, they not only learned about poverty in India, but also Skyped with Indian children who were "just like them" in an affluent, well-equipped school.

In this chapter, we examine Tenets 5 and 6 of transformative leadership, tenets that comprise two additional ideas introduced in the previous chapters:

- a focus on emancipation, democracy, equity, and social justice, and
- an emphasis on interconnectedness, interdependence, and global awareness.

These tenets offer some guidance for transformative leaders about how to transform schools. In fact, they suggest some additional criteria for making decisions about funding, hiring, curriculum, pedagogy, discipline, and many other policies and practices that comprise schooling. They suggest the need, as Sophie experienced it, for schools to make learning enjoyable, to help students acquire academic self-confidence; and they propose, as exemplified by Quiet Waters Elementary School, ways to expand the curriculum to enhance curiosity, critique, and global awareness.

In Chapter 1, I offered some questions educators could use to help make decisions—questions about who is marginalized, disadvantaged, excluded, and silenced and who is privileged, advantaged, included, or fully participative in any decision. By focusing on both the processes and potential outcomes of decisions, these questions attempt to direct attention to inequities and to those who are marginalized or excluded. The issues raised in Tenets 5 and 6 expand the conversation and provide some direction about the possible *content* of desired changes as well as some of the desired actions to help us accomplish our transformative goals. This is consistent with Torres's proposition that we need to advance both formal and

substantive democracy and that to do so, we must focus both on method (or processes) and on content (1998, pp. 148–149). This will help to promote what he describes as "radical democracy"—democracy that "postulates radical equality in racial/ethnic, class, and gender interactions, both at the level of the public sphere and in the intimacy of the household" (p. 149).

To this point, we have talked about the need to ensure that every student in every school feels included, welcome, and respected. We have also discussed the importance to civil society of an educated citizenry. But we have not emphasized the underlying *content* that makes these efforts a possibility. We have not emphasized the truths that if anyone suffers, we all suffer, or that if there is injustice anywhere, it is injustice for us, as well. In this chapter, therefore, we begin to respond to the question: How can we read the world, "act upon it, and if necessary, transform it?" (Macedo, 1995). Tenet 5 offers some bedrock principles for transformed schooling and argues the need for policy and practices to be centered on **emancipation, democracy, equity, and justice**.

Nancy Fraser (in Naples & Fraser, 2004) originally posited the need for both redistribution (that attends to economic injustice) and recognition (focusing on the cultural inequities) in order for transformation to occur. She urged that these analytical constructs be integrated, because neither one can be subordinated to the other. In the previous chapter we discussed redistribution—a rebalancing of priorities for public education and a redistribution of the hegemonic power structures that perpetuate inequity. In this chapter, we focus more specifically on what Fraser might call recognition—recognition of difference and of the multiple identities and perspectives that make up the glorious diversity of the world in which we live. We also implicitly refer to her third, political dimension of *representation*, added later to allow us to "problematize governance structures and decision-making

procedures" (p. 1117). This framework of redistribution, recognition, and representation helps to bring together the principles previously discussed and those still to come.

Bedrock Principles: Emancipation, Democracy, Equity, and Justice

To question the common belief that America is a land of opportunity is, as Pfaff (2010) notes in Chapter 3, often seen as heretical. Yet as events of the summer of 2015 clearly demonstrate, opportunities for health care, for recognition of love between LGBT couples, or for living and worshipping freely without fear of retribution or even assassination have not been equally distributed. Speaking in response to the June 2015 Supreme Court decision about same-sex marriage, President Obama began his address with the words:

> Our nation was founded on a bedrock principle that we are all created equal. The project of each generation is to bridge the meaning of those founding words with the realities of changing times—a never-ending quest to ensure those words ring true for every single American.

Obama went on to state, "When all Americans are treated as equal, we are all more free." Yet, unfortunately, we are still not all treated as equal, nor are we all equally "free." As times have changed, we have definitely seen advances in the freedoms accorded to some groups. Moreover, as Obama also asserted in that speech,

> But today should also give us hope that on the many issues with which we grapple, often painfully, real change is possible. Shift in hearts and minds is possible. And those who have come so far on their journey to equality have a

responsibility to reach back and help others join them, because for all of our differences, we are one people, stronger together than we could ever be alone.

One of the people who has lived her life, acknowledging continued injustices and reaching back to help others, is activist Grace Lee Boggs, who celebrated her 100th birthday the same eventful week in June as the Supreme Court decisions on housing rights, gay marriage, and healthcare in America.[1] Three years ago, she stated, "Because I was born to Chinese immigrant parents and because I was born a female, I learned very quickly that the world needed changing." Following receipt of her doctorate in philosophy from Bryn Mawr College, her quest for work was often thwarted as she was told, "We don't hire Orientals" (Chow, 2015). Subsequently, living in rat-infested housing, and working in Chicago for a subsistence wage, she came across a group of poor Black people protesting similar living conditions. This awareness was the beginning of her connection to the Black community, a connection that has become so deep and continuous that many, including the FBI, considered at times that she must be at least part Black. Married in 1953 to African American auto worker and activist James Boggs, she engaged in activism with him until his death in 1993. Wanting to "reinvent" herself, she began, in 2005, at the age of 90, writing a weekly column for the *Michigan Citizen*, a column she continued for eight years. Her work still not finished, she then "helped to start the James and Grace Lee Boggs School, a charter school that weaves Detroit—and its issues— into its curriculum" (Chow).

The centenary of Grace Boggs and the civil rights advances of June 2015 remind us of the continued need for emancipation, democracy, equity,

---

1   Unfortunately, since the time of writing, Grace Lee Boggs died on October 5, 2015.

and justice in this country and of the need for educators to ensure that these are central values of our public education system to ensure that we are all "more free."

Emancipation

Emancipation implies freedom from bondage and restraint, whether it be physical or psychological.

Emancipation may seem like a strange value with which to begin this discussion of Tenet 5, given its longstanding association with slavery. Moreover, I choose the word emancipation rather than the more common term "freedom" to emphasize that some people and groups in society are still, in some ways, in bondage, held captive by the chains of prejudice and discrimination.

Slavery is a practice many feel was eliminated in this country by Lincoln's emancipation proclamation of 1863, which asserted that all 3 million "persons held as slaves within any State or designated part of a State" should be "then, thenceforward, and forever free." To ensure the end of slavery, the Thirteenth Amendment was adopted in 1865, abolishing both slavery and "involuntary servitude." Nevertheless, as journalist Phillip Martin wrote in 2013, "If you think slavery ended in 1865, think again." Martin cited Luis CdeBaca of the State Department discussing human trafficking, saying:

> By the '80s and '90s, we were starting to see— whether it was Guatemalans, or Mexicans or others—suffering often in the same farms in the American South picking tomatoes, cucumbers, onions. So, when I had a chance to work on a farm worker slavery case, I didn't shy away from it. (2013)

Imagine the horror of being a farm worker on the same lands that once supported slavery! Yet, according to a report from anti-slavery.org, around 21 million people around the world live in some way in a form of slavery, with 60,000

estimated to be in the United States (Kristof, 2013). He writes:

> From women forced into prostitution, children and adults forced to work in agriculture, domestic work, or factories and sweatshops producing goods for global supply chains, entire families forced to work for nothing to pay off generational debts; or girls forced to marry older men, the illegal practice still blights our contemporary world.

Where in public schools today do students learn about human trafficking, the sex trade, or other sensitive and somewhat controversial issues? Why, in fact, do we permit statements that slavery was abolished more than 150 years ago to go unchallenged? Or, worse, how is it possible that Texas standards can eliminate any mention of Jim Crow or the KKK when the latter is a group that is still active today? Or how can they intentionally minimize the importance of slavery as a cause of the Civil War as was done in 2015, arguing instead that the war was fundamentally about states' rights?

Moreover, emancipation from physical bondage and servitude is only one form of oppression from which people need to be freed. If we take seriously the promise of "liberty" contained in the First Amendment, it is critically important to comprehend its full meaning. When we talk of liberty, are we simply referring to the ability to choose as in deciding whether to send our children to a charter school, a public school, or to home-school them? Are we talking about the ability to marry a person of our choice? Or are we including freedom from all forms of oppression, bullying, and discrimination?

In June 2015, in response to the horrible murder of nine African American worshippers in historic Emmanuel AME Church in Charleston, South Carolina, pleas were heard, and ultimately successfully, for the Confederate flag to be removed from the statehouse grounds; Alabama governor Robert

Bentley also quickly and quietly did the same. Georgia and Virginia took steps to remove the flag from their license plates; and several major retail outlets announced they would stop selling the Confederate flag. In other words, the tragedy precipitated action, at least in some places, toward a more complete emancipation, in that the constant and hostile reminder of slavery and racism was to be eliminated from view and, in part, from continued official sanction. In the debate, one often heard comments about the flag representing the "illustrious history and heritage of the South Carolina people." Yet, the fact is that 28% of South Carolina is Black and that the oppression and discrimination that group faced is not "represented" by the flag. Here one can see the real impact of the power held by a majority group in the state—power that ignored the heritage and emotions of approximately one-third of the population and that permitted the persistence of the flag until 2015.

But at the same time, evidence of hatred and racism also proliferated. Six Black churches in the South burned to the ground in the 10 days after the shootings at Emmanuel Church, with at least four of the burnings attributed to arson (Markus, 2015). In addition, Markus reported that, in the days following the Charleston murders, residents in at least six states found Ku Klux Klan recruitment flyers on their lawns.

The Charleston shootings clearly demonstrate once again the need for education to balance both public and private good. Despite the fact that one man admitted to the murders in Charleston, hate is not simply an individual passion, confined to the private domain. In fact, the shooter, despite acting alone, claimed he did so in the hope and belief that his actions would spark a race war. The import of the illustration is clear. The laws may be in place, but there is much work to be done in public schools to win the hearts and minds of young people so that ongoing repugnant incidents such as these are forever eliminated.

Thus conversations about emancipation must become part of the regular school curriculum. There is no place for such discrimination in a deeply democratic society; so until deep transformation happens, emancipation will not be truly achieved.

Democracy

Democracy—One person, one vote represents a thin and formal concept of governance in which the people, all of the people, make decisions that apply to all; whereas deep democracy recognizes the need for mutual benefit and diversity-respecting unity.

Democracy is another goal of transformative leadership. By this, I do not mean the formal democracy often referred to as "one person, one vote," although some of the recent legislative attacks on voting rights, and attempts to restrict people's access to the ballot box, make even this very thin and limited definition still salient. When I speak of democracy, I am not referring to a formal, institutional concept of democracy, but to Torres's (1998) substantive democracy and to Judith Green's richer and more expansive conception of deep democracy as mutual benefit, cited in Chapter 1. Green explains further, saying,

> Deeply understood, the democratic ideal is a normative guide for the development of diversity-respecting unity in habits of the heart that are shaped and corrected by reflective inquiry. (1999, p. 9)

To succeed, this ideal requires an education grounded in diversity, one that teaches students to critique and to reflect. It requires that schools attend to the creation of unity within diversity as they develop policies related to discipline, homework, bullying, and so on. Elsewhere (Shields, 2008). I have more thoroughly discussed how transformative leaders can democratize practice. I assert that schools are not, and should not try to be, democracies; however, their role is to teach students about, in, and for democracy in multiple ways. Students must start by learning *about* formal democratic practices, but their learning must be much deeper. They must be given opportunities to

practice democracy by learning to reflect and critique, to listen and to challenge, and to engage with others whose perspectives are different from theirs or those of their families. They must be put *in* various situations to learn to develop rules, to make choices, to understand how particular decisions and practices not only affect them, but others as well. Only then, are they educated *for* democracy—for full, active, and thoughtful participation in community life.

Democratizing Curriculum. Too often, as we talk about "covering the curriculum," or teaching to state standards, we imply that curriculum is the sum of the content to be communicated to students so they can pass standardized tests. However, as many prominent curriculum theorists (e.g., Grumet, 1995; Pinar, 2011) assert, curriculum is the ***conversation*** that makes sense of a topic. Moreover, conversation that pervades all aspects of the curriculum—the formal, informal, and hidden curriculum—is essential if we are to infuse the curriculum with democratic concepts and global understandings.

> To democratize curriculum involves opening it to the interpretations and perspectives of all students and their families and not simply presenting an authoritative orthodoxy.

These curricular conversations must become the norm. They are not simply nice pedagogical interludes that occur once the topic has been "covered" or the questions in the textbook answered correctly. They must be *the* way topics are introduced, expanded, and discussed in order to build understanding by connecting with the lived experiences of the students. In this way, the formal curriculum (that which is identified in standards and explicitly taught) may better reflect the lived experiences of every student in our schools.

For example, Denny, a young friend of mine, is a 13-year-old bi-racial child (Black and Hispanic), adopted by a single, White, gay male. As Denny grows from childhood, through adolescence to adulthood, and explores issues related to his own identity, how does he see himself reflected in the curriculum? How does he make sense of his heterosexuality and his father's homosexuality in ways

that lead him to deeper understanding and respect for both? How does he learn to critique the ways in which the dominant White culture has oppressed both African American and Hispanic males in our society, without becoming angry with his White father? What is his place in a still highly stratified and divided society?

Especially when his father seems uncomfortable discussing personal issues with his son, school must offer Denny a safe place to explore these and other questions, to examine the roles played by his Mexican ancestors in this country, to see strong, Black male role models, and to identify with his father's homosexual Caucasian culture as well. In a discussion of how educational experiences often act as a catalyst for the school-to-prison pipeline for minoritized youth, he must be free to wonder how his intersecting identities as an adoptee in a biracial family affect his life's chances.

If transformative leadership is to democratize practice, then there must be safe space for dialogue about the lived reality of every child and for the perspectives he or she brings. This includes the realities of social class, poverty, and homelessness, as well as issues of race, ethnicity, and sexual orientation. Too often, children are singled out and made to ask for special dispensation or a modified assignment if they cannot afford an assigned book or field trip, or if they cannot complete a task requiring particular material resources. No child, for whom poverty or homelessness is already a terrible burden not of their making, should have to raise his or her hand and ask for modifications because that, in itself, sends the message that school is not really for them. The requirement that every child read his or her electric meter over the course of a week and graph and analyze the data is, for example, impossible for some children. However, if the assignment had alternatives built in from the outset—the possibility to work in pairs collecting and graphing the data, or to work with a local business or the school caretaker, then children without a regular home could freely participate. Asking children to build a model of the Alamo or the solar system at home implies the presence of both parental assistance and materials from which to construct the model. The result is well known; children who have resources at home show up with an elaborately designed and erected model, while those without similar resources either pretend to have forgotten the due date or bring a much less "professional" looking assignment. One solution is to provide all children with the same materials at school and to require that they, and only they, be used to complete the assignment.

Anything we do that negatively singles out those who are less advantaged sends the message that school is not for them; and unfortunately many children receive this message repeatedly from the time they begin school in kindergarten. The alternative is for teachers to sensitively know the situation of their students and to provide choices that enable everyone, without exception, to complete class requirements—whether the class is at a pre-school or university level. For me, this message hit home one summer when a blind student enrolled in one of my seminars and I had to learn not simply to show a slide or PowerPoint, but to accurately describe the visual. I had to rethink group work so she could not simply act as a "participant observer" but truly participate, adding tactile components to some of my activities.

In thinking about curricular discussions about race, the situation of a fifth grade Muslim child I recounted elsewhere (Shields, 2012) comes to mind. When his class read a story that included a Muslim family, and engaged in a lively discussion about it, he offered to have his father come to speak to his class to explain some aspects of his Islamic faith. To the principal's dismay, criticisms soon rolled in—to both his office and that of the superintendent, complaining about the presentation, and particularly the father's assertion that Islam is

a religion of peace. In a truly transformed educational setting, there would not only be room for a discussion about Islam as a religion of peace, but for students to probe the terrorism of ISIS and to attempt to reconcile the two. This will not likely be very comfortable for the teacher who has no first-hand knowledge of Islam, no Muslim friends, and no training in facilitating dialogue about often-controversial issues. However, because suppressing dialogue is not the answer, the transformative leader will have to provide support and assistance to teachers to enable such conversations to occur.

Moreover, conversation is not only important for controversial topics but for meaningful learning to occur at all times and in every subject. As Pinar (2011) puts it, curriculum is a complicated conversation

> in which interlocutors are speaking not only among themselves but to those not present, not only to historical figures and unnamed peoples and places they may be studying, but to politicians and parents dead and alive, not to mention to the selves they have been, are in the process of becoming, and someday may become. (p. 43)

How different this is from our normal conceptions of curriculum, but how important for achieving the democratic goal of mutual understanding! Complicated conversations may benefit individual students as they find themselves included in the curriculum in ways that ensure they feel comfortable enough to express who they really are. They can finally speak without the need to censor their realities for fear of being shamed or blamed. This is also consistent with Parker Palmer's notion of education in which the subject, what he calls the "great thing" being studied, is at the center, and students bring their own experiences, knowledge, and questions to the exploration and meaning-making conversations. He explains:

A subject-centered classroom is not one in which students are ignored. Such a classroom honors one of the most vital needs our students have to be introduced to a world larger than their own experiences and egos, a world that expands their personal boundaries and enlarges their sense of community. (1998, p. 120)

This concept clearly suggests that conversation and dialogue are not add-ons, and certainly not limited to controversial issues, but central to the teaching and learning processes themselves. Curriculum as conversation, therefore, leads toward deeper mutual respect and understanding that benefits both the individual and society as a whole.

Equity

Equity, and not equality, implies the need for unequal and dissimilar inputs and supports for some individuals and groups to ensure more similar outcomes and outputs.

Equity as a guiding principle must undergird all of the decisions and actions of a transformative leader. As indicated by the foregoing discussions of emancipation and democracy, it is clear that treating all students in exactly the same way—whether in terms of discipline policy or curriculum requirements—is not the answer. Instead, as the illustration in Chapter 2 of the child needing two boxes to see the baseball game reminds us, sometimes unequal treatment is required in order for every child to succeed. This may mean additional time to complete an assignment, an allowance of 15 minutes to take a younger sibling to school before being counted late, a morning snack available in a cupboard below a microwave oven strategically placed in an open space, or permission for a student to quietly get up and leave a classroom when feeling overwhelmed.[2] It may

2   I am well aware of the legal issues here, but making arrangements for a time-out place, perhaps a library carrel or a visit with the school caretaker for a few minutes, can prevent serious inappropriate responses on the part of one or two students.

mean accepting Sophie's absence on "Welfare Wednesdays" and helping her to catch up quickly the following day.

In other words, it is critically important for the transformative educator to promote equity instead of equality within a school. Differential treatment for people with different needs or backgrounds, or differing strengths and weaknesses, is sometimes thought to be unfair and undemocratic, but nothing could be farther from the truth—as the children standing on boxes reminds us.

I recently watched a moving and inspiring interview with 33-year-old Nick Vujicic, born without arms or legs.[3] Although he needs assistance with every simple task, from eating to dressing himself, to moving from place to place, Nick has a rich life. Using a pointer attached to a strap around his neck and shoulders, Nick operates technical equipment; he graduated from college and holds down a full-time job. Although he cannot hug his wife or pick up his son, he enjoys a loving and supportive family life. Further he has traveled to more than 50 countries, speaking to groups of people about accepting and making the most of who they are.

Nick's success began in school, where, he tells us, he sat *on* his desk, while the other children sat *in* theirs. As the first child with no limbs to be fully mainstreamed into a public school class in Australia, there is no doubt that he needed considerable adaptation and assistance. Treating him exactly the same way as every other child would have been ridiculous. Yet, perhaps because Nick's need for unequal treatment was visibly obvious, and because he had a vivacious and outgoing personality, it did not seem unfair. Nonetheless, if every child and every group of children are to succeed, equity and not equality must be the underlying value.

---

3 One source of information about him is available at www.lifewithoutlimbs.org

Justice

Justice implies rightness and right outcomes according to the law. Although justice has moral overtones, moral action may go well beyond what is required for justice.

Only as transformative leaders identify emancipation, democracy, and equity as bedrock principles for the operation of their schools will they be able to claim they are operating a "just" school. In its origins, both from Latin *iusticia* and the old French *justice*, the word *justice* meant "uprightness" in accordance with right and fair principles, always with overtones of legality as well as moral rightness or ethical behavior, although morality is broader. One can imagine, for example, activity that is *moral*, and that goes well beyond what is required or "just"—a teacher paying for a student's field trip or buying her a new coat, for example. In some ways, whereas equity relates to the processes, to whether individuals are treated in ways that are intended to create the conditions for both a level playing field and for fair inputs and outcomes, justice relates to the outcome of collective, public good.

In education, leadership for social justice often makes reference to the works of Theoharis or Cambron-McCabe and McCarthy. Theoharis (2007), for example, defines social justice leadership as the meaning that

> principals make issues of race, class, gender, disability, sexual orientation, and other historically and currently marginalizing conditions in the United States central to their advocacy, leadership practice, and vision. This definition centers on addressing and eliminating marginalization in schools. (p. 223)

As Cambron-McCabe and McCarthy (2005) propose ways of preparing school leaders for social justice, they acknowledge that the concept is multi-faceted, contested, and, depending on the proponents, grounded in diverse perspectives. They assert, "The prevalence of social justice language in educational settings and scholarship

portends a new movement with as many meanings as actors on the scene" (p. 202). This begs the need, they argue, for "critical inquiry" for a re-examination of the norms and assumptions of schools that pose barriers to some students. And in 2007, when McKenzie and eight other scholars took up the same subject of leadership preparation, they identified three goals associated with leadership for social justice: a link with academic achievement, critical consciousness, and inclusive practices (p. 116).

In each of the above conceptions, individual academic achievement—as measured by standardized tests—plays a central role, as does the more collective notion of democratic citizenship. Sometimes, however, leadership for social justice seems to be used for activities that relate more to equality than to equity, more to injustice than to justice. A "three strikes" or "zero tolerance" discipline policy is sometimes deemed to be socially just in that it treats everyone in exactly the same way. Rigid applications of academic standards that result in the grade retention of many minoritized children are deemed to be socially just in that everyone must meet the same standard. Attempting to counteract this use of social justice that implies equality rather than equity, Bogotch and Shields (2012), who edited an international handbook, chose the title, *Educational Leadership and Social (In) Justice*. They believed that a focus on injustice would lead more naturally to an understanding of ways to counteract it and to deeper reflection about educational assumptions and practices that support and perpetuate injustice.

As we have seen, this is consistent with the plea issued by Gloria Ladson-Billings, in her address to the American Educational Research Association (AERA) on receiving the 2015 Social Justice Award. Dr. Ladson-Billings argued that the term "justice— just justice" is considerably broader than the concept of "social justice," and that a more expansive and inclusive term is necessary if we are to

address the many kinds of injustice in the world—economic and political as well as social. To these, one might add ecological, linguistic, geographic, and ideological as well. Dr. Ladson-Billings described three major forms of justice prominent in Western thinking (advanced by Mills, Nozick, and Rawls) and argued for adding concepts from non-Western thinking as well. In other words, she argued for an expanded focus, not simply on rules, but also on how they affect people's lives. She described how an emphasis on restorative justice as found in the South African Truth and Reconciliation Commission not only acknowledged the wrongs people had suffered but also gave people the opportunity to heal by acknowledging their responsibility in not speaking out, or not trying to stop atrocities.

The key, she argued, is that, in addition to other prescribed learning objectives, children regularly learn the foundations of injustice in schools as they encounter hostility, prejudice, and discrimination that goes unchallenged and a curriculum in which injustice is largely ignored. A focus on justice—just justice—would raise everyone's awareness of the vulnerable in our society as well as look to the potential and possibilities of the future. It would help everyone in our schools and society to acknowledge the underlying injustices (related to disparities such as race, gender identity, religion, ability) that are perpetuated by the systems of privilege in which many educators participate and from which we benefit. This learning may occur in literature as one discusses, for example, the racism inherent in Mark Twain's (1884) *Huckleberry Finn*, in science, as one examines the causes of climate change, or in math as one graphs locations of toxins in the air related to various neighborhoods and their economic status. In other words, once again, teaching about injustice can be incorporated into every subject rather than seen as a time-consuming and intrusive add-on. In sum, social justice education may be (and I would

argue must be) woven throughout the curriculum as a whole.

"Justice" Education

In education, many people think about a socially just education as one in which all students are enabled to perform equally, in which the achievement gap on test scores is eliminated and, hence, in which all students have been successfully educated to the same level on the same standards. In some ways, this is what may be called a socially just education. In contrast, a "social justice" education is one in which the ideas of extending the educational experience to explore, understand, and be able to address the wider global inequities is perhaps closer to Ladson-Billings' notion of "justice—just justice."

Too many educators have uncritically accepted the educational myth that in this country, schools are just, that everyone has an equal opportunity to succeed, and that education provides the opportunity for social mobility. To this point, this chapter has demonstrated the need for education to address both injustice experienced by individuals and by the collective in order for the possibility of a more radically and deeply democratic society to be realized. It has shown there is still a deep-seated need for emancipation, democracy, equity, and justice to provide a solid foundation for a mutually beneficial democratic society. Yet, to truly transform education, helping all students feel welcomed, included, and respected in our schools and in our society is only a beginning. It is also necessary to prepare global citizens, caring, compassionate, and knowledgeable individuals who are aware of our interdependence and interconnectedness with others across the globe.

Transformative educators must choose. They must consciously examine their positionality and privilege and opt for what Ladson-Billings called the "heavy lifting" of understanding our own culture, of identifying injustice, and of addressing it. Martin Luther King is often quoted as saying, "Injustice anywhere is a threat to justice everywhere." For that reason, transformative leaders must not only identify and critique injustice at home but also abroad,—and understand it, engage with it, and learn to address it. It is no longer sufficient to claim to live in the best country in the world (a claim shared by those who live in other countries such as Canada and Finland as well). Global peace and prosperity are essential for the welfare and the future of all. This leads to Tenet 6: an emphasis of transformed schools on **interconnectedness, interdependence, and global awareness**.

Interconnectedness: Relationships as a Building Block

> Interconnectedness reminds us that we do not live in a vacuum and that what happens in one location affects what occurs elsewhere. It focuses on relationships and reminds us that how we behave can have a profound impact on other people.

Interconnectedness occurs on several levels: individual and collective, local and global, current as well as historical. There is little doubt that as individuals, we come into this world, connected by an umbilical cord to another human being who has sustained us and given us life. On a collective level, the phrase "it's a small world," has come into common parlance, indicating the ways in which we are connected to one another, not just individually, but as groups, and as nations. Moreover, as numerous people have pointed out, the past is inextricably connected to the present and the future. This is the point made by Bakhtin (1981), who argues the need to live in what he calls "biographical time." He asserted the importance of taking into account the historical forces that have shaped our belief systems, our cultures, and our world, but also of accepting that these facts must constantly be reinterpreted through new and more accurate lenses.

To address our need for interconnectedness, *relationships* must be placed at the center of the educational experiences—relationships between

teacher and students, between students and students, and between students and the subject matter to be studied. We are well aware that the mantra for a real estate agent selling a house is "location, location, location." Fewer educators are conscious that one mantra for educators could be "relationships, relationships, relationships." Relationships, therefore, undergird the sixth tenet: **the need to focus on interconnectedness, interdependence, and global awareness** and not simply on academic achievement or test scores.

Individual Connectedness

People live and learn in relation to others. Gabriel (from Chapter 2) may never have realized his potential had my friend not established a supportive and caring relationship with him. Sophie would never have become a teacher had she not encountered an instructor who encouraged her and made learning enjoyable. Nick Vujicic would never have developed into a secure and loving adult, able to sustain a career, a marriage relationship, and to be a caring father had he not had the support of his family, friends, and teachers. Moreover, I am sure most people can think of one caring, supportive, and interested teacher who made a difference for them, perhaps someone who helped them understand their own value.

In the previously mentioned interview, Nick recalled that during one speech he was making to a full auditorium of students, the audience silence was suddenly broken by one student weeping audibly. When he invited her to the stage, she hugged him tightly, tearfully explaining that it was the first time anyone had told her she was valuable and lovable. This should never happen in our schools. All children must receive the message repeatedly from every adult whom they encounter that they are valuable and worthy of respect.

I think of Gwen, a former 7th grade student of mine who lived in a dormitory in a remote Labrador village. Gwen had an older sister who lived in the village and a younger brother who lived in a different dormitory. One day, when Gwen was missing from class, I asked the principal if he knew anything about her absence. When he indicated she was in the hospital, I dropped in to visit her after class. She explained that, after spending the evening with her sister and her friends, she had missed curfew at the dormitory. Disbelieving her story and wondering if perhaps she had been abused, the dorm parents had requested she be kept overnight at the hospital. My visit lasted perhaps half an hour, but created an enduring bond between us. A few years later, when Gwen came to visit us in a new town, we realized she was not far from two younger siblings whom she had not seen for many years and soon we were able to reconnect them. Still later, she spent time with us getting acquainted with my two young children. And now, 40 years later, I anticipate her cheery message in my email every year on my birthday. And all of this occurred because I took half an hour to visit her that day after school.

As a university professor, I still consistently attempt to develop strong and positive relationships with my students, recognizing how much I learn from them, as they hopefully learn from me. To do so, I require weekly journals, to which I also respond weekly, in which students discuss understanding and reactions to readings. The ensuing dialogue and deepened relationships make the extra effort worthwhile for all of us. I also generally hold at least one class in my home accompanied by food—another excellent relationship-building strategy. When I taught high school, the focus was a little different in that my students did not generally come to my house; however, I did develop assignments that helped me to get to know them. I have contravened school policy and left my classroom door unlocked before school and over the

noon hour for students to "hang out" and, often, to interact with me. I have used responses to student journals to reassure students of their worth. In other words, I have tried to learn multiple ways to both develop relationships with students and to show them respect.

You are likely aware of the phrase, now a movie title as well as a game, "six degrees of separation." The concept is that anyone in the world can likely be connected through a network of six relationships to anyone else. And as impossible as that notion may sound at first, it has been taken seriously by scientists and psychologists for the past hundred years. Studies of social networks, such as those conducted by Gurevich in a dissertation written at MIT in 1961, or by Kochen, an Austrian mathematician, or American psychologist Stanley Milgram—all took up what came to be known as "the small world problem." Although there is little empirical proof that the number of connections is always six, there are definitely studies that demonstrate the importance of relationships to human development.

We have long known, for example, the importance of human touch for health and well-being. From the monkey studies in which baby monkeys favored warm, cloth-covered surrogate "mothers," to studies in orphanages where babies were either left on their own in cribs or held and cuddled while being fed, we have learned the importance of interaction. More recently, the phrase "skin hunger" has become an accepted medical term to emphasize the human need for touch. Similarly Naisbitt and Naisbitt's (2001) book *High Tech, High Touch* popularized the need to understand technology through a human lens.

Sometimes one hears of schools in which the reform initiative has been aimed at ensuring that every child has at least one positive interaction with a caring adult every day. This is ridiculous. Positive interaction with a caring adult should be the norm in every classroom and every school in

the nation. No child should, like Gabriel, have to wait until he or she is almost 16, finally encountering by luck someone who cares. No child, like Sophie, should internalize the message that school is simply "babysitting" her. One role of the teacher is to be a caring advocate for his or her students; no special program should be necessary.

In fact, one of the most important aspects of education is the interaction with other human beings. Otherwise, information dissemination could occur in huge lecture theaters or only through technology. This is one reason I fear for students being educated in certain kinds of alternative schools in which they follow "individualized curriculum" provided on computer screens. In fact, this is a misinterpretation of "individualized curriculum." It should not simply mean assessing the student's starting point and providing sequenced, computerized instruction from where they are. It must also include conversations and dialogue in which children make sense of the material through conversations that relate to their own background and interests. High quality curriculum cannot simply be delivered solely through individualized technical approaches.[4]

Sometimes today we hear the concept "personalized" curriculum. This may be an improvement, in that it emphasizes the person's interests and abilities, instead of simply having them work individually on a set of standardized activities. In other words, individualization implies similar objectives for all learners, selected and determined through standards committees and the like, yet delivered individually, while personalization at minimum

---

4 Please don't misinterpret this point. I am not arguing against online instruction, which I know from personal experience can be extremely interactive and effective, successful at fostering meaningful learning, strong interaction, and personal relationships. I am arguing against any form of educational pedagogy that does not foster interconnectedness and "conversation to make sense of things."

requires that the learner have some input into the creation of his or her learning goals or schedules. At the same time, we must always remember that unless we focus on how we are connected one to another, we are failing to balance public and private good in education.

Wider Interconnectedness

Recall how a volcanic eruption in Iceland grounded airplanes flying to many European cities, including London, Paris, Amsterdam, and Brussels, for eight days in 2010, stranding thousands of passengers worldwide. Think about how the world was riveted to the television day and night in March 2015 after the suicidal crash of a German plane into the Alps with passengers from at least 15 countries aboard. Recollect how Union Carbide's gas leak in Bhopal, India, in 1984 resulted in legal proceedings in both India and the United States. Or reflect on the numerous vitriolic statements attributing the rise of the terrorist Islamic State to either the Bush administration's involvements in the Middle East or to President Obama's subsequent withdrawal of American troops. What occurs in one part of the world is inextricably linked to what occurs elsewhere. Thus, the interconnectedness and interdependence of our world, economically, ecologically, as well as socially and politically are of considerable import and must be central to both the formal and the informal curriculum.

Internal and international tensions in the last few decades have increasingly resulted in dislocations, in people having to leave their homes and countries with the result that other regions often decry having to bear the "burden" of an influx of displaced peoples. Too often, this results in economic hardship, in new conflict, and in the unfortunate deaths of those trying to escape persecution and worse at home. Consider those who have died in small boats awaiting permission to land on foreign shores. A recent Amnesty International

report (June 2015) titled *The Global Refugee Crisis: A Conspiracy of Neglect* reported that in 2013 more than 50 million people worldwide were "forcibly displaced from their homes" (p. 5). The report goes on to discuss how lack of international support for the countries receiving these refugees had resulted in discrimination, hardship, and death for many refugees as well as increasing pressures on destination countries. For example, Syrian refugees surge into Lebanon at a rate of approximately 2,500 a day, exacerbating an already challenging situation for Lebanon, a small country that struggles to support the more than 400,000 Palestinian refugees who have earlier found their way across the border. Mudallali (2013) states that the "political impact of the crisis is pushing Lebanon to the brink" (p. 1), exacerbating cultural, economic, and educational pressures.

Amnesty International reports, "In April 2015, more than 1,000 people died in the space of ten days while attempting to cross the Mediterranean" (p. 6). The following month, newspapers worldwide reported the plight of refugees and migrants from Myanmar and Bangladesh who were floating in boats "left without food, water, and medical care for a week" and then pushed back to sea by countries refusing to accept them. Continuing into the fall of 2015, the ceaseless exodus of people from troubled areas led to emergency summits of countries attempting to address the unprecedented situation. The increase of economic pressures is, unfortunately, also accompanied by a normalization of xenophobia and racism. And all of this occurs despite the United Nations Refugee Convention, intended to protect displaced persons.

There are numerous other areas related to the economy and resource production that could be discussed and connected to typical lessons in geography, social studies, or science as well as activities in art and music classes. The recent spate of hydraulic fracturing (fracking) has, for example, brought considerable prosperity to previously depressed

rural areas of the country, but also brought with it incredible pressures on local housing and education, as well as increased tensions as "newcomers" have "invaded" once relatively quiet and homogeneous communities. Changes in education standards, to which reference has already been made, are undoubtedly a boon to textbook publishers but put incredible pressure on already fiscally taxed school systems.

On a more human and cultural level, one might rejoice that the Supreme Court has put an end to marriage discrimination in this country, but sympathize with school districts, universities, and other organizations who may have their already strained budgets stretched even farther as more people are (rightly) entitled to full benefit packages.

Moreover, interconnectedness occurs on many levels. Nationally, the apparently random killing of a woman on a San Francisco pier sparked renewed calls for tougher immigration enforcement, possibly affecting thousands of immigrants, largely from Mexico and Central and South America. Internationally, the pressures placed on the European Union by the Greek default on its loan had fiscal repercussions throughout the world. The list of situations that come to mind is endless and the importance of increasing this kind of understanding cannot be overstated.

Historical Interconnectedness. Bakhtin (1981) says that the past must always be reinterpreted in the light of the present, as we acquire new insights and incorporate new perspectives. Moreover, he argues that if we view the past as "authoritative" and therefore unchanged and unchanging, it leads to an unquestioning acceptance of the status quo, to regarding the way things are as the way they should always be. A fixed interpretation of the past closes us to the possibility of new understandings and ways of thinking. He asserts:

> The authoritative word is therefore ... organically connected with a past that is felt to be hierarchically

higher. It is, so to speak, the word of the fathers. Its authority was already acknowledged in the past ... therefore authoritative discourse permits no play with the context framing it, no play with creative stylizing variants on it. It enters our verbal consciousness as a compact and indivisible mass, one must either totally affirm it, or totally reject it. (pp. 342–343)

This view of history as fixed and authoritative helps to account for the fierceness of the South Carolina debate about the Confederate flag. Nevertheless, the emotional appeal of Republican senator Jenny Horne in which she rejected the notion of "heritage" in favor of reinterpretation that would remove a "symbol of hate" is an illustration of how being open to new interpretations can effect change. In her brief, four-minute speech she stated, "I'm sorry, I have heard enough about heritage. I am a lifelong South Carolinian. I am a descendant of Jefferson Davis." She then pleaded: "I cannot believe that we do not have the heart in this body to do something meaningful such as take a symbol of hate off these grounds on Friday." Her speech is thought to have turned the course of the debate and, hence, of history (Truong, 2015). Despite the fact that Jenny Horne's grandfather was president of the Confederate States during the Civil War, she was open to the needed reinterpretation that would permit a new vision of history to replace the old, to permit healing to begin.

Similarly, the previously mentioned furor about new Texas state educational social studies standards that have eliminated mention of the Ku Klux Klan or Jim Crow, and have relegated "slavery" to a tertiary cause of the Civil War, reflects the need to understand the past. Without an understanding of the past, and how its events influence the present, change is unlikely to occur. The volatile conversations about the use of the Confederate flag are purported by some to be about honoring the valor of

those who fought for the South; they emphasize that the flag is representative of Southern history and heritage and not of hatred and racism. The lack of awareness of interconnectedness is stunning. The population of the South is not simply White. What history is being celebrated? How can a society that fought to retain slavery assert that the history is not racist? Witness the racist language of the Texas Ordinance of Secession, cited by sociologist James Loewen.[5] The Texas Ordinance of Secession, adopted by the Secession Convention on February 1, 1861, by a vote of 166 to 8 included the following statement:

> We hold as undeniable truths that the governments of the various States, and of the confederacy itself, were established exclusively by the white race, for themselves and their posterity; that the African race had no agency in their establishment; that they were rightfully held and regarded as an inferior and dependent race, and in that condition only could their existence in this country be rendered beneficial or tolerable. (Texas Ordinance, 1861)

This is one excellent illustration of the need to understand historical and vertical, as well as lateral, interconnections. It is not possible to understand current situations without understanding the roots of those sores that still fester today.

All of these examples demonstrate the interconnectedness that we must acknowledge and learn about in our public schools. But transformation must go farther. It must acknowledge that interconnectedness is only a beginning. We are truly interdependent and must therefore learn to develop trust in one another, despite our differences.

---

5   He made these comments during an appearance on *The Diane Rehm Show*, July 8, 2015.

Interdependence: A True Mosaic

In previous sections, we have made mention of concepts such as a school-to-prison pipeline or the challenges of impoverished children in our schools. We may shake our heads in dismay at the continued evidence of negative police interactions with Black youth and applaud the rise of the Black Lives Matter movement. We may feel a temporary tug at our hearts when we read that more than 700,000 children die each year from lack of clean water or that 67 million children worldwide do not have the opportunity to attend school. But what, really, does this have to do with us?

Interdependence suggests not only that we are affected by what happens elsewhere, and that our behavior can profoundly affect others, but that we are dependent on what occurs elsewhere. Our very welfare and survival depend on social and economic reform that, as some would say, raises all boats and not just yachts.

> Interdependence goes beyond interconnectedness, because it asserts that our very welfare and survival depend on what occurs elsewhere.

Let's take a simple example: children living in poverty in American urban areas, such as Detroit. For the most part, adequate food and nutrition are rarely available to those who live in poverty in urban ghettos. In recent years, there has actually been much discussion of how to remedy what have come to be known as "food deserts"—areas that lack access to affordable fruits, vegetables, and other healthy foods. Lack of proper nutrition makes it more difficult to concentrate and, hence, to perform to an academically high standard. It may also lead to theft and even to more serious crime. Further, because of the high rates of urban crime, many inner-city children and youth have personally experienced violence and loss. Detroit, for example, experienced 14,500 violent crimes—murder, rape, robbery, aggravated assault—in 2013, and a rate of 45 murders per 100,000 people—the highest in the nation (Abbey-Lambertz, 2014). Moreover, the extent and repeated nature of this violence contribute not only to post-traumatic

stress on the part of many children but also to chronic post-traumatic stress.

When schools have many children suffering chronic distress, the overall achievement may be lowered, thus suggesting to those not in a similar situation that it is time to move, to permit their children to attend "higher-performing schools." In Detroit, we have seen how a cluster of social and economic factors has led to dramatic decline in the public school population. The smaller tax base, thus, negatively affects the resources and facilities of the district, further exacerbating unsuccessful outcomes and a negative reputation, and once again, discourages many people from enrolling their children. Those remaining in the public schools are, for the most part, people who feel they have little choice—no ability to move and no resources to pay the fees or to fulfill the parental participation requirements of many charter or private schools. This situation affects everyone. The less ability the city has to provide services, the higher the residential taxes become, the greater the exodus from urban areas, and the larger the decline in school enrollment. The more the schools decline, the less qualified the workforce, the more unemployment, the greater the crime rate, the higher the court and incarceration costs, and so on.

Yet, the tendency is, once again, to engage in deficit thinking and misplaced assumptions, to place blame on those experiencing poverty and trauma, without going any further. I recently heard an articulate group of teenagers involved in an urban leadership project explain that when they attended school, they knew they did not have the money their peers did, they realized they could not regularly attend movies, participate in school events, and so on, but they thought that there was simply something wrong with themselves and their families. They did not understand, they said, until their involvement with the community program, that poverty is socially constructed,

evidence of unequal and unjust distribution of power and wealth in our society.

Teaching Interdependence

This is the kind of conversation missing in many of our schools—we support individualistic notions of education and private good but ignore the interdependence of all. A study by Westheimer and Kahn (2004) of different kinds of school programs shows clearly:

> Programs that successfully educate for democracy can promote very different outcomes. Some programs may foster the ability or the commitment to participate, while others may prompt critical analysis that focuses on macro structural issues, the role of interest groups, power dynamics, and/or social justice. (p. 262)

I agree with Westheimer and Kahn, and with Dr. Law, principal of Quiet Waters School in the introduction to this chapter, that it is important for students to understand how people and events are both interconnected and interdependent if we are to correctly analyze and resolve the many challenges of modern life. Thus, we must think differently and more broadly about curriculum.

For example, school children are often taught the three "R's"—not reading, 'riting, and 'rithmatic but reduce, reuse, recycle. The Green Cup Challenge, sponsored by the Green Schools Alliance, encourages children to "measure and reduce energy use, improve recycling and waste reduction programs, and promote water conservation" (Green Cup Challenge, 2015). Blue boxes and recycle bins have appeared in every major city in the country, with cities increasingly assuming the cost of recycling. Indeed, recycling has sometimes been touted as the solution to greenhouse gas reduction and the ecological salvation of our planet.

Yet, as well intentioned and important as recycling is, it is rare that discussions include any sense of the interconnectedness of recycling with the cost of global energy production or commodity costs. Rarely is there discussion of the fact that, in some jurisdictions, adopting recycling programs adds cost rather than being a means of making a profit. The moral import of the decision as "the right thing to do" is rarely emphasized. This also has implications for where recycling programs exist, where other disposal such as landfills are located, and so forth. On the website of the Green Schools Alliance, there are lists of ways that individuals, families, and organizations can reduce use, but there is no discussion of the interrelated issues. For example, the reduced value of recycled commodities can be attributed, at least in part, to the strike of American West Coast port workers that resulted in backlogs of goods, as well as to the recent reduction in global oil prices. When oil prices decline, it becomes less desirable and less profitable to make articles of recycled plastic rather than to create new items. In turn, this new production affects the generation of greenhouse gases that affect the environment and the price of recycled commodities, and so on.

It is therefore critical for 21st century students to develop a kind of global curiosity and to understand our global interconnectedness as well. Mahbubani (2013) writes that instead of thinking about the world in terms of 7 billion people living on 193 separate boats (the number of countries in the world), we need to think about it as 7 billion people living in 193 separate cabins on the same boat. What happens in the neighboring cabin affects our ability to both enjoy the voyage and to reach our destination. We need to ask whether the resources of the boat can support 7 billion people, whether it can take on an infinite number of new passengers, and about the potential "comfort" of each. We may need to create policies limiting the number of passengers or governing the equitable distribution of food.

To do so, we will also need to understand how subsidies of agricultural products in one country affect the availability and price of food in another (as in Haiti's experience with the cost of rice); how a healthcare epidemic in one country affects medical research and development in another (as in the 2015 Ebola crisis and the search for a cure), or how a political crisis in one country can affect the politics of others (witness the rise of ISIS or the change of government in Afghanistan). The examples are endless. The point is that transforming the focus of democratic education, as Dr. Law did in Quiet Waters Elementary School, is essential for our modern world. Moreover, his intent was to help students see that those who live in other countries are both like and unlike us. Except perhaps in times of crisis (and even then with caution), they do not need a hegemonic missionary focus on "being helped," but one of standing alongside and working together to steer the boat toward a better future for all.

Moving Forward

In the previous chapter, we identified the need to balance an emphasis on both private and public good. In this chapter, we have emphasized the collective and interdependent nature of our world, and the need for our education system to ensure that education is not a solitary activity. We have urged an end to educational benefits that accrue only to certain privileged individuals who acquire knowledge, skills, and attitudes to enable their success. Education is the foundation of a healthy, prosperous, and sustainable civil, democratic, and global society. The exploration of each foundational term identified in Tenet 5 as bedrock principles of transformative leaders and of transformed organizations, and of the broader, global values that comprise Tenet 6 has begun to demonstrate how schools may be reconstructed in transformative ways, addressing

policies, as well as curriculum to ensure inclusion of multiple perspectives. As we have seen, each principle is a contested concept needing exploration and enlightened understanding; but, in combination with each other and with the other tenets, they do provide some principles that may guide change processes.

In the next, concluding chapter, we will examine the final two tenets of transformative leadership and explore how, taken holistically, transformative leadership can undergird significant and sustained change in education.

Transformation Underway

Public education does not need any more managerial leaders. It does not need another round of technocrats or placeholders. Public education needs transformative leaders, leaders who are willing to ask and answer difficult questions. Children need educational leaders who are willing to create deep and meaningful change that will benefit all students. In considering their needs, I remind myself that we, as educators, choose to participate in the current system. We decide to walk through the front doors of our schools each day. We must remember, however, that our children do not make those same choices. We compel them to attend school. Their choices are directly limited by their zip codes. Indirectly, these choices are a result of their socioeconomic status.

I have been a school administrator for nearly 20 years now ... I have been working to examine the underlying beliefs and tacit assumptions ... I have been critically interrogating my own belief systems and the

resulting actions ... To be successful, school principals need to encourage and develop others to become transformative leaders as well. ... The reality of continuous and sustainable school improvement is that, in spite of external pressure and increased political scrutiny, educators—not politicians—remain solely responsible for creating learning environments that are conducive to academic achievement.

To engage in truly transformative leadership is exhausting. It is complex. As a school principal I understand that I am a product of the very system I seek to change.

What I have realized is that I am going to have to re-think a few of my non-negotiables at this one moment in time. I am going to have to be willing to stretch existing relationships, create tensions in an otherwise calm environment, and find spiritual strength if I am going to challenge the status quo that I helped create. ... I accept the reality that I still have so much real work to do, because there is so much promise to realize. (Bieneman, 2011, pp. 221–235)

The premise of transformative leadership theory is that it provides guidance for educators as to the transformation necessary to ensure that schools offer more equitable, inclusive, and socially just learning environments for all students. That this is true is captured in the excerpts from a chapter written about leadership by a truly transformative leader, Dr. Paula Bieneman. In her chapter, she captures both the promise of transformative leadership and the hard work required to effect its promise. She identifies the need for Tenet 7, **critique and promise**, that reminds us of the need for both thoughtful critique and promising improvement—for critical reflection and transformative action to accomplish our goal; and she draws on the final principle, Tenet 8, **the need for moral courage**, that undergirds all else. She acknowledges that although transformation is exhausting, continuous, hard work, it is also a moral imperative, given that although we, as adults, have chosen to be educators, our students have not necessarily chosen to attend our schools.

In this chapter, therefore, we examine these final two tenets as we explore what it takes to be truly transformative, what school leaders need, and what they can do as starting points to transform their schools. As we examine the premises of the final two tenets, we will investigate what it might mean to prepare others to be transformative leaders who offer promise both to our students and our wider society. We will examine the need, described by Bieneman, for spiritual grounding that permits us to identify and challenge our non-negotiables. We shall identify some possible actions a transformative leader may take to create a deeper sense of community within the school, and to begin the task, with his or her whole staff, of equitable transformation. And we shall understand how moral courage is difficult and sometimes dangerous, how it requires educators to become advocates, sometimes activists, and, almost always, public intellectuals.

Critique and Promise

Critical leadership theory—The distinguishing feature of any critical theory is that it focuses on the least advantaged and least successful in our society and attempts to both explain and to rectify their inequitable situation.

Transformative leadership is a critical leadership theory. This is one of the features that distinguishes it from most other leadership theories identified in Chapter 1. It thus responds to Foster's call, with which the first chapter began, for a critical theory of leadership, one he hoped would "be critically educative," one that does not "only look at the conditions in which we live" but decides how to change them (1986, p. 185). Recognizing that we are complicit, that, as Bieneman states, we have helped to create the inequitable and often hostile conditions of our schools, we must challenge the very underpinnings of this system and begin to transform it.

Understanding Critique

Critique, not to be confused with criticism or with critical thinking, implies assessing the merits (the advantages and disadvantages of something), again with the implicit need to deconstruct disjuncture between interpretation and fact.

Critique is not a synonym for negative and unproductive criticism; nor is it synonymous with "critical thinking." Critique comes from a Greek word meaning "skilled in judging" and implies a thoughtful examination of the merits of something; hence *critique* requires the transformative leader to develop and exercise skill in judging what is working and what is not working to fulfill the deeply democratic purposes of public schooling.

Critique includes the concept of "deconstruction," often attributed to French philosopher Jacques Derrida. Reflecting on his experiences of alienation growing up in French-colonized Algeria, Derrida's deconstruction focused on the imposition of a foreign language as *the* language of instruction. Deconstruction recognizes that it is *our* interpretation of reality, *our* language, and *our* texts that need to be deconstructed, because new understandings are what permit us to influence action in new directions. Deconstruction emphasizes the dichotomy between fact and interpretation and, hence, also draws on Freire's (1970) distinction between reading the word and reading the world. Critique, as a philosophical concept, has been extensively discussed by such prominent thinkers as Kant, Hegel, and Marx, and has, as Biesta and Stams assert (2001) "become intimately connected with the question of education" (p. 58) from the period known as the Enlightenment onward. Hence, thoughtful examination of the status quo has led to what have become known as *critical theories.*

In reality there are multiple critical theories—but all begin by seeking the emancipation and liberation of the least powerful, the most marginalized in our society. Hence, there are critical race theories (Collins, 1991; Lynn & Parker, 2006), critical queer theories (Capper, 1998; Sears, 1993), critical feminist theories (Ellsworth, 1989; Kenway & Modra, 1992), and so on. Sometimes, the term *radical* instead of *critical* is used as in radical post-structuralism, which focuses on a critique of structures that inhibit the full participation of everyone, or radical post-modernism, which focuses on a critique of how the concept of inexorable progress ignores those who are downtrodden in the process, and so on.

Each focuses on a specific group that has been disadvantaged and dispossessed under our current systems. In the latter half of 2015, the Black Lives Matter movement is attempting to mobilize society around a critique of current police practices vis-à-vis Black Americans. It seeks to demonstrate how unequal power relations and inherent prejudice and discrimination have historically resulted in inappropriate and excessively hostile and aggressive action against those like Trayvon Martin, or Sandra Bland—and these represent but the tip of the iceberg. This is one form of a critical approach that seeks to decrease domination and to increase freedom for a particular group in society.

The aim of transformative leadership is broad: to increase school success, emancipation, democracy, equity, and justice for all groups of students who experience marginalization, including those who are racialized, who are poor, LGBTQ, from a non-dominant religious or language group, or who experience physical or mental challenges, and so forth. Transformative leaders attempt to critique and redress positions and perspectives, structures and cultures, policies and practices that result in any form of disrespect or inequity. No wonder school principals find it exhausting!

Transformative leaders must critique the beliefs and assumptions that perpetuate deficit thinking and the implicit values that perpetuate racism and homophobia. They must address religious persecution based on inappropriate tacit assumptions; deconstruct policies such as admission to AP classes or gifted programs or zero tolerance discipline policies; and ensure that both formal and informal curricula do not disadvantage those who are impoverished or whose home language and culture are different from the language of instruction. They must ensure that anti-bullying programs do

not simply focus on individual behavior but deconstruct the underlying social constructions that perpetuate feelings of superiority or inferiority that often underlie student behavior. They must create inclusive and just learning environments in which all students can develop intellectually and also learn to live in harmony together despite their differences.

This is complex. There are no easy answers. For a transformative leader, critique is not univocal, it is not dogmatic, it does not necessarily pre-suppose a right or a wrong answer, but it always raises questions and assesses the responses in terms of some underlying principles regarding who is excluded and who included. What is important here, however, is that the criteria themselves are subject to deconstruction, reflection, and change. Critique always acknowledges that there are multiple perspectives, but it inherently focuses on the notion of promise and possibility. Biesta and Stams (2001) posit that deconstruction

> tries to open up the system in the name of that which cannot be thought of in terms of the system (and yet makes the system possible). This reveals that the deconstructive affirmation is not simply an affirmation of what is known to be excluded by the system. It is an affirmation of an otherness that is always to come ... Deconstruction is an openness towards the unforeseeable in-coming. (p. 68)

Critique, therefore, implies possibility and promise, hence, the dual focus of Tenet 7.

Emphasizing Promise

Promise implies hope, possibility, and future action. It implies a contract in which educational leaders undertake to serve their constituency—*all* members of their school community, as expressed in the opening words of the U.S. Constitution, "We the people." It does not state, "We the White people" or "We the rich people," but simply "the people."

Promise, as both verb and noun, implies action to which one is committed as well as the concept of outcomes that fulfill that promise. In other words, it emphasizes the probability of achieving the hopeful and positive potential of an assured course of action.

Educators, especially those in public schools, supported by all taxpayers, must take seriously the question inherent in Rousseau's concept of social contract: How can we be free and live together?

Promise sees the potential in each and every child and offers the possibility of a better future. Coleman and Shaw-Coltrane (2015) remind us that when Lewis Terman, psychologist and early developer of IQ testing, studied gifted children, he not only tragically "eliminated many potentially bright youngsters of low economic and immigrant status," but he also "failed to find two future Nobel Prize winners who were in school at the time of his study" (p. 71). Discussing the wisdom of Dr. James Gallagher, another prominent educator and child psychologist, Coleman and Shaw-Coltrane assert:

> Underrepresentation of culturally different children stems from a complex combination of societal, economic and political, and personal factors (Coleman & Gallagher, 1995; J. J. Gallagher, 2006). It is a pervasive and pernicious problem. Underrepresentation is a "tragic waste of human potential: the concerto never written, the scientific discovery never made, the political solution never found" (J. J. Gallagher & Kinney, 1974, p. vii). It is an individual heartbreak—but it is also a societal tragedy. (p. 71)

To counteract this "tragic waste of human potential," transformative leaders must offer promise to all (not just to a few identified as special)—promise of action to counteract the inequities and injustices of the education system; promise to open to those who are culturally different all of the opportunities and resources of the school; promise of a safe, secure, and inclusive learning environment for each child free from shame or blame; promise of the opportunity to develop one's individual intellectual potential; and to have the prospect of participating fully in our wider democratic society. Unfortunately, whether or not these promises are fulfilled is too often

dependent on children's environment, family backgrounds, zip codes, and so on. Too often, schools in high-income zip codes act as private schools, responsive to parents' wishes, offering considerable advantages to those already privileged by their social status. Too often, schools in impoverished areas are under-resourced, pay teachers lower salaries, and offer fewer learning opportunities to their students. The fact that there are fewer electives, fewer advanced classes, and fewer fully qualified teachers in impoverished urban or rural schools denies opportunity to those who also have the fewest resources outside of school.

The status quo is backwards. It is unacceptable and unjust. In a just society, should not social and educational institutions offer the most advantage to those who have the least? We need a new contract—a new promise of hope and possibility for the most vulnerable children in our society. And in our schools, we need curriculum, pedagogy, policies, and practices that offer the promise of windows of opportunity to better futures to all of our students.

Promise implies action. To ensure we are both free and live together in harmony, we make and uphold promises. When we make a promise to someone, it suggests that in safety and in mutual benefit, we will hold fast to a particular course of action. If we promise to take a child to a movie or to the circus, we are honor-bound to fulfill the commitment. Educators, in many states, take an "oath," and solemnly swear (or affirm) to "support, obey and defend the Constitution of the United States and the Constitution of [this] State" and to "discharge the duties of my office with fidelity"; sometimes, the last words change to "discharge the duties of a teacher" or of an educator. In each case, we are, in fact, promising to uphold the promises of equality and equity inherent in these documents, to ensure the promise of the preamble that "we the people" undertake to uphold the constitution *in order to* "form a more perfect union."

As discussed previously, a more perfect union involves providing individual opportunities and freedom, but it also demands a more "perfect" collective union, living in harmony and in mutual benefit, with one another. Unfortunately, the concept of community has often been interpreted narrowly and exclusively, and can lead to misunderstanding and mistrust rather than to the peace and prosperity for all promised in the constitution.

Living in Community

Community is, therefore, another contested term, another shifting signifier, as academics like to call it. Dictionaries tend to define it, first, in terms of place—people living in a common locale. The Old English word for community was *gemaenscipe*, which relates to the German *Gemeinschaft* used by the sociologist Tönnies to describe a simpler, friendlier past era in which people knew and worked with their neighbors, respected tradition, and emphasized kinship and shared experience. In this kind of community, there is a nostalgic focus on the past, on taken-for-granted relationships and assumptions of homogeneity, and on predictable commitments and behaviors. Unfortunately, in our nostalgia, we often ignore the concomitant emphasis on stereotypical recognition and labeling of others that led to what Thayer-Bacon (2001) claims is a vulnerability to community. She writes:

> All knowers are vulnerable to harm from their social communities, ranging from mild physical or psychological abuse to the extreme pain of exclusion or expulsion from the community. Young and new knowers are extremely vulnerable to harm and have very limited ways of protecting themselves. Knowers who represent minority, dissenting voices are also more vulnerable to harm. If the community members are young children, they have probably not developed their own voice yet,

and they do not have a way of protecting themselves from physical or emotional abuse. (p. 7)

Gemeinschaft communities are not confined to locales but join people who are like-minded, often in exclusionary and sometimes hostile ways. Members of a church comprise a community, as do members of social clubs, private clubs, golf and country clubs, and associations such as the National Rifle Association or the American Heart Association. Each is formed because of a common bond of belief or interest among its members.

Tönnies identifies an opposing view of community he called *Gesellschaft*. Merz and Furman (1997) explain: "In *Gemeinschaft*, an individual's status is determined by familial and cultural roles; in a Gesellschaft, status is determined by the job that a person does, based on competency and training as well as the place of the job-role in the organizational hierarchy" (p. 16). Although this may represent a more cosmopolitan and more diverse community, it is still an inadequate concept for the pluralistic and complex groupings of people today in public spaces, either in civic locales or in schools. Elsewhere I have offered the concept of a *community of difference* as an antidote to the more traditional view of community. A community of difference is similar to what Thayer-Bacon calls a pluralistic community in which members

> embrace a pluralistic commitment to the value of having our community be open in its membership, so that there are no insiders and outsiders, and all have the possibility of belonging and contributing to the constructing of knowledge. A pluralistic commitment means we embrace and value differences among our knowers. (p. 10)

In a community of difference, everything is negotiable—except respect for one another, and principles of inclusion, and justice (also to be determined). The term *community of difference*

Community of difference refers to a community in which different perspectives are included and respected, and in which everyone together, determines the guiding principles and norms of the group.

acknowledges the need for social cohesion, but not for assimilation or domination. It recognizes the need to develop agreements about shared values, common beliefs, and preferred practices, but not to coerce others into accepting predetermined historic concepts.

The concept is, therefore, both normative and descriptive. It necessitates sensitivity to private advancement and to the public good, to how the inequitable distribution of power can become oppressive and exclusive and, hence, to redistribution; it requires acceptance of conflicting beliefs and cultural values; and it entails a commitment to opening oneself to the Other, to listening, and to learning—to extensive and time-consuming dialogue that leads not necessarily to agreement, but certainly to respect and understanding.

A community of difference, founded on inclusion, and goals of respect and social justice is qualitatively different from two other common approaches to community often found in schools, in that its roots, like those of transformative leadership, are critical perspectives. One common term, popularized by DuFour, Guidice, Magee, Martin, and Zivkovic (2002, 2012) is that of a *professional learning community* (PLC). This notion of a learning community counteracts the notion, advanced in classical management theory, that a few people at the top should do all the thinking for the organization, because the rest are "too stupid" (as Taylor would say) to think for themselves. In a PLC, all professionals contribute to the community. Recently, the concept of a professional learning community has found its way into the everyday parlance of educational leaders, where, in some jurisdictions, it has become a mandatory reform strategy. The problem (of course) is that too many iterations of professional learning communities are narrowly focused on "student success" as defined by test scores to the exclusion of all of the other components of an excellent and inviting learning environment. Learning communities

are intended, it appears to me, to respond to Sergiovanni's (1994) assertion that schools should be more like communities than organizations; hence, they call for clarity of purpose, for collaborative action, for a focus on continuous improvement and on results. Once again, as in many leadership theories introduced in Chapter 1, there is, however, no clear mandate for equity or social justice. DuFour et al. (2002), for example, assert that "the success and well-being of each student will be the primary focus of the student support department of the future" (p. 25), again ignoring the important public good goals or sociological factors important in student "success" more broadly defined. Moreover, professional learning communities inherently focus on the professionals— the teachers and what occurs within the school, neglecting the impact of the wider social, cultural, and economic forces that impinge on students. Too often, communication is still only one way in that "the counselor contacts the parents and advises them of the team's recommendations" (p. 27) without asking for input in return.

Similarly, communities of practice comprise "an accumulation of skills and information" that lead to "becoming more competent in the community's practices" (Wearmount & Berryman, 2012, p. 255) and from which "'brokers' transfer understandings and procedures across boundaries" (p. 255). Once again, the one-way communication of information seems increasingly problematic, given the diversity of most organizations and the growing need for dialogue among members. In contrast to this focus on developing norms and practices and communicating them to those less expert, I find Martin Buber's concept of a community of practice to be more appealing in that it is a community in which each participant is open to an "adventure in heightened awareness of living"—a concept consistent with the openness and dialogic approach of a community of difference.

In 1993, Tierney wrote a book titled *Communities of Difference*, in which he described his vision for higher education in the 21st century, that comprised a "postmodern" concept of community. In his foreword to the book, Giroux wrote that the concept of "community of difference" "crosses disciplinary boundaries and fashions new connections and insights," and that it is aware of the "interconnection between difference, power, and ethics." Giroux goes on to state that difference

> is always treated historically and relationally as a struggle over power, signs, and identities ... theory is a practice that is constantly informing one's beliefs, actions, and practices ... it is also a borderland where conversations begin, differences confront each other, hopes are initiated, and social struggles are waged. (pp. ix–x)

This is the kind of community transformative leaders are called to create—one founded on conflict as well as hope, on critique as well as promise. This kind of community struggles over the meaning and the implementation of redistribution, recognition, and representation. These communities, like all the work of transformative leaders, are never finished, never static, and always changing, always becoming; they are what Maxine Greene (1973) describes as "pluralistic communities always-in-the-making" (p. 267).

Moral Courage

Moral courage involves an agreed-upon set of values and actions, including both ends and means, that focus on doing the right things for all members of the school community, ensuring all are included and respected, despite possible resistance.

To implement this vision of a community of difference grounded in emancipation, democracy, justice, and equity, transformative leaders will have to draw on the moral courage identified by Tenet 8. Although each of the other tenets requires a courageous approach to leadership, it is once one arrives at this point, having considered all the aspects advanced by this theory, that one realizes how very

difficult it can be to lead for transformation. Challenging the status quo, as Bieneman in the introduction to this chapter notes, is not easy. It brings into play all of the conflicting beliefs and power positions of members of the school community as well as all of the external pressures and increased political scrutiny under which leaders operate today. It acknowledges that leaders not only experience the mandate for deep and meaningful transformation, they are "products of the very system they seek to change."

Thus, we can challenge our beliefs and assumptions, deconstruct them, recognize the aspects that perpetuate inequity and injustice, and even become aware of some ways to begin to effect change, but if we do not have moral courage, we will be reluctant to act. We will retreat into our fears and insecurities, our discomfort with conflict, and our need to be liked and to remain secure. This is perhaps why Palmer (1998) titled his seminal book, *The Courage to Teach*. Teaching and leading in authentic and relational ways always require courage.

Mohan (2011) cites former Attorney General Eric Holder, who, in 2009, called the American people "essentially a nation of cowards" (p. 55) because we are afraid to advance more than our "own, narrow, self-interest." He stated, "It's a question of being honest with ourselves and racial issues that divide us ... It's not easy to talk about it. We have to have the guts to be honest with each other, accept criticism, [and] accept new proposals." And this is exactly the problem.

Education has too often kowtowed to those who are vocal, to those who already have power, to those who do not want change, fearing that opening opportunities in school to "those kids" from less advantaged or immigrant groups, or to those with "alternative lifestyles" will result in fewer opportunities for their own (already advantaged) children. Transformative leaders must be fiercely courageous. They must not only talk, but act. They must, as we heard Weiner (2003) assert earlier, insert an "ethical as well as a political discourse back into the language of education," make visible and confront the "mechanisms of power and domination" that structure the policies, curricula, and practices of schools in ways that continue to stratify students and perpetuate unequitable outcomes.

Starting Points

This call to courageous action likely rings true for those for whom transformative leadership resonates and who are passionate about improving schools for all students, especially the most marginalized and least successful in our current systems, but the question on all lips is likely, "Great, so how do we start? What do we do on Monday morning?" And of course, my initial response is that there is no prescription and that there are no easy answers. What the leader does in any given environment is dependent on his or her unique context, on the specific challenges of the community, on the awareness and readiness for change of the membership, and his or her own dispositions and commitments. Nevertheless, in this section, I will try to give some suggestions about starting points and activities that can act as a catalyst for the kind of transformation we have been discussing.

Spiritual Grounding

Bieneman (above) suggests that transformative leaders need to be spiritually grounded. This is incredibly important. By spiritual, I am not talking about having a formal religious belief or affiliation, although for some, spiritual grounding does come in large part from this affiliation. By spiritual, I am referring to what Parker Palmer (1998) refers to as "the diverse ways we answer the heart's longing to be connected with the largeness of life—a longing that animates love and work" (p. 5). Starratt (2005) uses different words but expresses the same idea

when he defines spirituality as "a way of being present to the most profound realities of one's world" (p. 67), in which we offer to one another what he calls the *spirituality of presence*. He identifies three ways in which this spirituality operates— by affirming, critiquing, and enabling one another. To offer a spirituality of presence requires that we begin by treating one another with absolute regard, affirming each person's inherent worthiness and value. This requires critique and the promise of presence—that we engage in self-critique, appraising ourselves "as the cause of a blockage to authentic communication" and appraising what, in others, may block "our mutual ability to communicate authentically" (p. 77). An enabling presence "empowers others to be themselves" (p. 82).

In fact, empowerment is a key outcome of transformative leadership in that individuals and groups are freed, that is, empowered, to participate fully in democratic society, freed from the constraints of exclusionary practices and stereotypes, to be who they truly are. Once this emancipation occurs, empowered people are able to join in collective action to bring about change, to act without fear of reprisals, and to have their voices heard.

The starting point, therefore, as stated at the outset, is ourselves. What do we believe about others? How do we communicate value, respect, and absolute regard? How do we enable others to be their authentic selves, to bring the fullness of their identities and lived experiences into the place we call school and into the conversations required for deep learning and understanding? Moreover, how, as Bieneman asks, can we also help others to do the same?

Non-negotiables

If we are spiritually grounded, we know our bedrock principles; we are aware of what guides us, what grounds us, what we stand for, what we will negotiate, and what are our non-negotiables. In other words, we understand, at the outset, when and where we can compromise and where compromise may absolutely not be appropriate. In this regard, the ancient wisdom of Sun Tzu is helpful. Despite the fact he was a military commander (and schools are certainly not military organizations), his aphorisms have much to teach educators. For example, his advice to know when to fight and when not to fight (545BCE/1972, 3.17) is reminiscent of the more familiar saying, "Choose the hill you wish to die on." Sometimes we have to build alliances, retreat and regroup, float some trial balloons, and so forth. But these must be tactics in the overall strategy to attack inequities, rather than continuous excuses. In section 5, statement 5, Sun Tzu states, "indirect methods will be needed in order to secure victory." In other words, transformative leaders cannot simply tell people they are wrong. It is important to help people discover meaning for themselves, perhaps through an examination of data, or by means of extensive dialogue about an issue.

Regardless of how "non-negotiable" our positions, Sun Tzu offers additional advice that is worth remembering: "When you surround an army, leave an outlet free. Do not press a desperate foe too hard" (7.36). If we are treating people with absolute regard, we will never leave them in a position of total defeat or desperation. Whether we are dealing with a faculty member whose position differs from our own or a student who is acting out, leaving a place for dignified "retreat" is essential. If we destroy the respect or confidence of another, we will never win them to our position; they will shut down, dig in, and fail to engage in any kind of interaction or dialogue that may lead to changed understanding and enlightenment.

Some Key Strategies

Thus, firmly grounded in one's beliefs and self-knowledge, and cognizant of the need to act

courageously, yet strategically, the leader is ready to begin. Two important starting strategies are the examination of data and the use of widespread dialogue. Each requires extensive deliberation and consistent use, although here our discussion can barely scratch the surface of each technique.

Examining Data

Data do not only comprise facts and figure but also include perceptions and feelings, beliefs and values—anything that people believe to be real.

Although there are many excellent leaders who use data as a basis for conversations that change perceptions and, hence, practices, here I will use the example of Dr. Paula Bieneman, whose words began this chapter. One of the strategies used repeatedly by Bieneman and other successful transformative leaders is to bring data to the table for extensive examination and discussion. She writes that one starting point for discussion is

> the achievement gap between white and non-white students, low-income and non-low-income children. The path of least resistance is, and always has been, the provision of services to remediate the child's perceived deficits, rather than to question the effectiveness and efficacy of the institutionalized practices. (2011, p. 223)

The point made here is important. Transformative discussions use data, not to focus on the individual child's achievement or lack thereof but on trends and patterns that identify institutionalized beliefs and practices that must be transformed.

Hence, principals bring to the table overall school data and ask such questions as previously raised: Who is succeeding here and why? Who is not succeeding and why? Often, in these discussions, teachers will resort to previously entrenched positions, repeating the common wisdom that, for example, the "parents of the African American children just don't care; they do not come into the school, and they do not support their child's homework." Here the leader must persist, asking for alternative explanations. On one occasion, Bieneman informed me that at this point, she usually plays the devil's advocate and gives examples of other children, perhaps White children, who come from single-parent homes, or whose parent she knows is mentally ill, or who is poor, and asks why they are succeeding.

One year, she identified that in her school of approximately 500 students, 100% of the behavioral referrals came from 25% of the students, the large majority of whom were African American. Thus, she determined these were data she needed to take to her staff. She explains that together, they use data to "change curriculum, to determine who needs intervention, and generally make decisions about what they are going to do." On one occasion, Bieneman reported a fascinating conversation to me; she told me that she had spent considerable time trying to have her teachers identify reasons for disparate achievement results in the school, only to have been told repeatedly that the problem was with the motivation of the children and not within their control as educators. In frustration she had said to her teachers:

> Okay if everything we're doing is fine and it's just the kids, I'm going to have some banners made with the data that say, "At our school we're proud that 85% of the white kids meet in reading and math, 50% of the black kids meet in reading and math," ... I'm going to put those up publicly. You're going to see it when you walk in the main door.

Of course, she was not serious but was trying to make a point with her teachers. When they objected, "You can't put that up," she responded, "Well, why not? If that's the best we can do, let's just own it, embrace it, make it public." Good principals use every strategy possible to help teachers accept their responsibility for creating positive learning opportunities and environments for all

children and for teaching in ways that ensure that all children succeed. Moreover, she recognized that there always needs to be someone raising questions, pushing, asking if what is happening is "good enough" or if there is something more they should be doing.

Free-writing. One strategy that works well to get all teachers involved is that of free writing. Dr. Bieneman uses this at every staff and grade-level meeting. She poses a question such as, "Why are only 50% of our African American students achieving when 85% of White students meet standards?" and asks teachers to write for five minutes. Sometimes, they exchange papers and share anonymously in large groups; sometimes she collects the responses, collates them, and uses them as a basis for discussion at subsequent meetings. She explains that although at first teachers resisted having to write, they soon began to approach her with challenges, asking if their own questions might form the basis for collective thinking and writing at the next meeting.

Another principal uses a variation of this strategy at every meeting, giving all of her teachers a packet of post-it notes and asking them to add comments regarding issues and discussions to a large board divided into four categories (kudos, critiques, concerns, questions). She, too, collates all responses and sends them out within minutes of the meeting's close via email for teacher reflection and subsequent discussion at daily planning meetings.

In every case, the point is to establish ongoing reflection about the data available within the school. This prevents personal attacks or blaming individuals and encourages collective thought and action. Interestingly, this is also consistent with the first step established in an extensive national program in New Zealand. There transformative leadership theory is combined with Kaupapa Maori (Maori traditional knowledge) and other critical concepts to effect reform of schools to

---

Free writing is a strategy by which people brainstorm in silence and then use their written expression of their thoughts, either anonymously or with identification, as a basis for reflection and dialogue.

enhance the success of all students, with particular emphasis on Maori students. In this extensive program of reform the first step is called "profiling," in which school leadership teams develop school profiles that identify equities and inequities in multiple areas, including student performance, as a basis for reflection and conversation.

Dialogue Is Key

Dialogue implies an openness to others, a "flowing through" of ideas, and not a percussive attempt to win points as in discussion, concussion, or percussion.

Another strategy, perhaps the key strategy, transformative leaders will use to bring about change in perceptions and beliefs that leads to transformative action is that of dialogue. As has been said frequently, dialogue is not just talk; in some ways, as others have expressed (e.g., Bakhtin, 1984; Shields & Edwards, 2005; Sidorkin, 1999), dialogue is a way of life. It involves listening as much as talking, wanting to understand instead of always seeking agreement, and always being open to new perspectives, new ideas, new ways of thinking. It involves both communicational and relational skills that, as Thayer-Bacon posits, must acknowledge differences and the influences of contextuality; it "must be humble and cautious, and not assume that it is right" (2001, p. 17). In other words, dialogue is always relational, aimed at deepening our mutual understanding of one another and the issue at hand. Bakhtin, philosopher and literary critic, writes, "The truth is not born and does not reside in the head of an individual person; it is born of the dialogical intercourse *between people* in the collective search for truth" (1984, p. 110), and later in the same work, he repeats the idea: One voice alone concludes nothing and decides nothing. "Two voices is the minimum for life, the minimum for existence" (p. 213).

Thus, Bakhtin argues that only as an idea comes into contact with what he describes as "other, *foreign*, ideas" can it come to reality. He argues,

Human thought becomes genuine thought, i.e., an idea, only under the conditions of a living

contact with another foreign thought, embodied
in the voice of another person, that is, in the consciousness of another person as expressed in his
word. (1973, p. 71)

The concept is that dialogue is absolutely essential for making meaning and for bringing new
ideas to life. It is not an add-on; it is not something
one does if there is time, but must actually be the
starting point for transformation. Yes, promoting
and engaging in dialogue takes time. It must be
planned thoughtfully, although the dialogue itself
must be spontaneous, building on the interplay of
everyone's ideas. Here, the transformative leader
must understand that the time spent up front in
challenging, deconstructing, and reconstructing
mental models and conceptual frameworks is
essential for transformation. Moreover, dialogue
takes considerably less time than undoing an
unsuccessful policy or approach once it has been
implemented.

Meaning-making with teachers. For that reason,
the leader must rethink how business is conducted
in the building. Every staff meeting, for example,
should begin with some kind of dialogic activity,
whether a think-pair-share, a quick 10-question
survey to be discussed, a free-writing activity fol-
lowed by discussion, or a critical incident posed as
an open-ended problem. Images or a story or a
research article, a letter from a parent, a newspaper
clipping, or data from a recent test—all provide
the basis for dialogue and reflection about who is
being disadvantaged or excluded and who is being
privileged and included and what, together, they
can do to redress the inequities. The "answer" will
not necessarily be forthcoming in any one brief
discussion, but what is key is that issues of equity,
inclusion, and justice be kept before the staff at all
times. When the transformative leader models
this approach, then other informal discussions
and smaller meetings of departments or teams of
teachers are much more likely to adopt similar

practices—especially if these practices are embedded in the daily expectations and conversations of the school.

This must become a priority. Conversations about inclusion and justice cannot be left to the end of a busy agenda; they must not be displaced by an "important" policy discussion or a "critically important" request from a superintendent, and so on. It must be apparent from the outset that the goal of equitable transformation is not confined to empty words but is a concrete goal that is held front and center in the mindset of everyone in the school.

Another reason why ongoing dialogue is so important is that the community is always changing; new teachers are being added and some leave; the student and parent population changes yearly as some graduate and others begin their journey; policies and curricular guidelines from district and state are also often transitory. Hence, the conversation must always be renewed. At one point, Paula Bieneman wondered, for example, why the math scores they had worked so hard to raise had started on a downward trajectory. As she examined the data, she became aware that she had increased her staff by almost 100% and so, although she had not thought about it before, she realized she "essentially had to start over with all the dialogue." Hill (1991) describes the necessity of continued dialogue in this way:

> Marginalization will be perpetuated if new voices and perspectives are added while the priorities and core of the organization remain unchanged. Marginalization ends, and conversations of respect begin when the curriculum is reconceived to be unimplementable without the central participation of the currently excluded and marginalized. (cited in Tierney, 1993, p. 25)

Because the context is never static or stable, continuous and ongoing dialogue is essential to continued successful and sustainable transformation.

Meaning-making with students. If we want teachers to employ interactive, dialogue strategies with students, transformative leaders must model these strategies at every turn with teachers. However, sometimes we still hesitate to employ the concept of curriculum as conversation, cognizant of our own shortcomings and vulnerabilities. Sometimes we use the students as excuses, saying that they are not ready to handle discussion of sensitive topics. But in general, the students see through us. They not only recognize the need for dialogue but also attribute its lack to teachers' reluctance and even fear. Mohan (2009) reports that when she interviewed students about their school experiences, one stated:

> I think teachers are too afraid to talk, to be the first person to talk with their students about race and culture. And unless it is in your textbook, you don't learn about it, because teachers are still afraid to step outside of the box in that category because they're too afraid to step on anyone's toes, get in trouble, offend anyone, that they just teach you exactly what's in the history books and what's in the history books, we all know, is just the generic what they want you to know about history.

Throughout the interviews Mohan conducted, as numerous students re-iterated the need for dialogue, their comments were laced with words and phrases like, "taboo," "silence," "afraid to step outside of the box," "hurt someone's feelings," "get in trouble," "too PC," and "say the wrong thing."

Students are perceptive. They recognize our lack of moral courage and our reluctance to engage with controversial topics. No wonder there seems to be a lack of moral courage in the wider society to advance justice, if today's students lack the role models in schools to point the way forward. Until and unless educators develop the courage to speak, we will remain at the level of critique, failing to introduce actions that can lead to the promise of significant transformation. Thus it is crucial that the transformative leader model that both dialogue and transformation are priorities before moving to relevant other business.

Keeping Interruptions in Perspective

Sometimes school leaders talk about their work as "putting out fires." Transformative leaders, however, with their clear sense of moral purpose and moral courage organize their day so that what matters is at the forefront of their activities. They do not permit interruptions and emergencies to consume all of their time or energy or to crowd out the important dialogue about inclusion and equity or essential actions to create a just learning environment.

That said, emergencies do arise and important interruptions occur regularly. A student is lost or injured, a custodial parent is frantic because a non-custodial parent has picked up a child after school, the superintendent pays a surprise visit with a local politician, and so on. And, of course, each of these must be addressed. For this reason, transformative leaders need some strategies for dealing with interruptions to ensure they do not co-opt the important work of transformation.

One strategy, of course, that must be emphasized is the importance of setting agendas for meetings strategically, with an activity supporting and framing the social justice agenda at the outset. Starting each meeting with free writing or dialogue as discussed above will ensure that issues of equity are foregrounded and that everyone recognizes their importance to attaining the overall goals of the school.

Another Metaphor: Building a Fire Escape

Weick (1996) draws on lessons learned when 13 expert firefighters lost their lives fighting an out-of-control wildfire in Mann Gulch. He argues that

just as firefighters need to know when to advance and when to escape and how to do so, so too do educational leaders. Thus, he identifies five propositions that comprise lessons we might learn from the three surviving firefighters. First, he posits that we need to "appreciate the complexity of small events and mobilize complex systems to sense and manage them" (p. 568). We cannot ignore what appear to be small isolated events or micro aggressions in our institutions. We cannot ignore deficit or derogatory statements made by students or teachers. And we cannot ignore disparate test scores by identifiable groups of students. Each must be addressed on the spot. Each of these small "fires" can smolder under the surface and suddenly escalate to threaten the life of the organization.

Second, Weick suggests, "Effective firefighting occurs when people know what they do not know and simultaneously trust and mistrust their past experience" (p. 569). Transformative leaders must always be conscious of what they do not know, always aware of hidden prejudices and blind spots, and always willing to learn from one another. Past success does not predetermine current success in a school in which demographics, ideology, and dominant powerful players have changed. Third, Weick suggests that effective leaders need "models for rogue events" (p. 570). This is similar to Margaret Wheatley's assertion of the need to discover underlying patterns and, hence, pressure points. It is not sufficient to focus on isolated events; it is also necessary to determine their relationship. Who are the powerful players? Who are the angry or docile ones? Who is feeling most disaffected and marginalized and whose parents have the power to exert pressure on the central administration? These and numerous other questions may help school leaders to understand who is supportive of given change, and to build a coalition that may counteract pushback and negativity.

Weick's fourth proposition is that we need to "manage issues rather than solve problems" (p. 571).

Here I agree that we cannot "solve" every problem that arises, and that problems do not "stay solved" in that new unforeseen consequences often accompany the best "solutions." Nevertheless, the phrase *managing issues* does not ring true to me as it could easily suggest a brushing aside, or hiding, or ignoring the very issues that must be addressed through courageous dialogue and action. I would rather suggest, once again, that challenges must be taken up and confronted through dialogue that leads to multiple perspectives, new ideas, and a possible, if temporary, new course of action.

Finally, Weick states the importance of "putting into place a system of lookouts, communication, escape routes, and safety zones (LCES)" (p. 571). In some ways, this is the most important proposition. Having lookouts, knowing who is on board, who is an ally in the important justice work is of immeasurable benefit. Having the support and assistance of other like-minded people prevents the exhausting work from being overwhelming; it makes possible the seemingly impossible. It enlists allies in the work of communicating the goals, in identifying areas of needed change, in ensuring that dialogue is both multi-directional and continuous, and in garnering the power of collective action. Escape routes remind us of Sun Tzu's aphorism to ensure everyone can maintain a dignified exit. Cornering people is never productive; similarly, letting oneself be cornered is, similarly, dangerous. Having put in place lookouts and many lines of communication helps to avoid being blindsided.

And finally, every transformative leader needs a "safety zone," a place where he or she can relax and be renewed, people with whom you may share your doubts and insecurities. Leadership can be a lonely and arduous activity and the challenges of transformative leadership multiply and exacerbate both the excitement and the difficulty. For this reason it is critically important to develop a network of like-minded and critical friends who will advise, support, and encourage you in the process.

Looking Ahead: Transformative Leaders and Public Intellectuals

In this examination of transformative leadership, we have taken as our starting points the fact that the educational playing field is inherently inequitable (in that it reflects and often supports the inequities in our wider society) and that it is the role and responsibility of educators and perhaps in particular of educational leaders to be active and involved in their redress, to accept the mandate for deep and equitable change. And I have suggested that transformative leadership, with the eight tenets I list here again for your convenience, offers guidance for truly transforming (not simply changing) our schools to become more inclusive, equitable, and socially just. It is a critical theory that can truly effect transformation if we accept

1. a mandate for deep and equitable change
2. the need to deconstruct knowledge frameworks that perpetuate inequity and injustice and to reconstruct them in more equitable ways
3. the need to address and redress the inequitable distribution of power
4. an emphasis on both private and public (individual and collective) good
5. a focus on emancipation, democracy, equity, and justice
6. an emphasis on interconnectedness, interdependence, and global awareness.
7. the necessity of balancing critique with promise, and
8. the call to exhibit moral courage. (Shields, 2013)

We have discussed the need to transform knowledge frameworks, to redistribute hegemonic power, and to prepare students both for individual excellence and for democratic citizenship. We have also identified the concepts of emancipation,

democracy, justice, and equity that must undergird the ways in which we think about policy, pedagogy, and practice. Additionally, the tenets emphasize the necessity for global curiosity and awareness that help us to understand the interconnectedness and interdependence of our world.

Finally, we have stressed that this work is difficult and exhausting and most definitely requires moral courage. In sum, transformative leadership calls us to a new way of life, one in which these principles pervade everything we do, one in which we cannot help but speak up and work for equity and justice in our schools, communities, nation, and, indeed, our world. The word *transformative* itself rhymes with the word *live* and, thus, perhaps suggests a new way of life. In fact, it calls us, as educators, to become what some might call public intellectuals. Hitchens (2008) states that "to be a public intellectual is in some sense something that you are, and not so much something that you do" (¶2). He went on to say, "Many scholars are intelligent and highly regarded professors, but they are somehow not public intellectuals," and I believe the same could be said of many school-based educational leaders. To be a public intellectual requires that we help to promote "enlightened understanding" (Bode, 2001) wherever we are by encouraging and facilitating the participation of the general public in dialogue and debate about conflicting ideologies; by presenting alternative and relevant interpretations, strategies and solutions; and, hence, by making a difference.

In the wake of all of the violence (by police and other individuals who engaged in mass shootings) that occurred in America in the summer of 2015, numerous commentators began to talk about the need to increase the national focus on mental health, to identify problems early, and to find ways to prevent the violence. Although this is definitely important, public intellectuals should also facilitate conversations about more controversial issues, such as how the challenges related to inadequate food or housing, lack of affordable healthcare and

A public intellectual has "one foot in the contemplative world and another in the political" (Melzer, Wineberger, & Zinman, 2003, p. xi). One speaks authoritatively and publicly about one's domain of expertise.

insurance coverage, deepening debt loads, inequitable school and university graduation rates, disproportionate incarceration rates, and the perpetuation of income and power imbalances in a nation result in too many people feeling desperate and hopeless, seemingly without recourse except to resort to violence. Certainly an increased emphasis on mental health would be a good thing, but it will never counteract the impact of other injustices that deny the promise of education to be the "great equalizer." This is consistent with Pierre Bourdieu's argument (1977) that "the primary contribution of social scientists to society is to illuminate the mechanisms of domination and to show how these mechanisms reproduce social inequities, thus making the social sciences inherently critical" (p. 29).

This was the lesson learned by Zak Ebrahim, son of one of the 1993 World Trade Center's bombers. He recounts: "Growing up in a bigoted household I wasn't prepared for the real world. I had been raised to judge people based on arbitrary measurements like a person's race or religion." He asks the important question, "So what opened my eyes?" And he continues to explain that during the 2000 presidential election campaign, he was invited to participate in the National Youth Convention in Philadelphia. He states:

> One day, toward the end of the convention, I found out that one of the kids I had befriended was Jewish. ... I realized that there was no natural animosity between the two of us; I had never had a Jewish friend before. And frankly I felt a sense of pride in having been able to overcome a barrier that for most of my life I had been led to believe was insurmountable ... I was able to contrast the stereotypes I had been taught as a child with real life experiences. ... Inspiration can often come from an unexpected place. (Ebrahim, 2014)

Zak learned that hate could be replaced by love, that rejection could be supplanted by acceptance.

And perhaps, he can teach us that schools, in which students can experience respect, inclusion, acceptance, and success, can be that surprising and unexpected place of inspiration and experience that replaces the stereotypes and beliefs sometimes taught in homes and other institutions in society.

Whether the transformative leader is illuminating mechanisms of domination within the school, or in a wider and perhaps more public forum in the local community, tremendous moral courage is required. Edward Said (1994) posits that the role of the intellectual

> has an edge to it, and cannot be played without a sense of being someone whose place it is publically to raise embarrassing questions, to confront orthodoxy and dogma (rather than to produce them), to be someone who cannot easily be co-opted by governments or corporations, and whose raison d'être is to represent all those people and issues that are routinely forgotten or swept under the rug. The intellectual does so on the basis of universal principles: that all human beings are entitled to expect decent standards of behavior concerning freedom and justice from worldly powers or nations, and that deliberate or inadvertent violations of these standards need to be testified and fought against courageously. (p. 9)

That is, indeed, the raison d'être of the transformative leader—to "represent all those people and issues that are routinely forgotten or swept under the rug." That does not mean it is the only task of the transformative leader, for, as we have stated previously, there are numerous daily activities, including raising test scores, budgeting, personnel management, scheduling, community building, and so on, that transformative leadership does not explicitly address. But if schools are to be sites of transformation that offer opportunity for all children, we cannot focus solely on routine and technical issues.

In New Zealand, there is a saying, "What is good for all students is not necessarily good for Maori; but what is good for Maori is definitely good for all students." Here we could state the same thing. What is good for all students is not necessarily good for those who are marginalized and disenfranchised; but what is good for the marginalized and disenfranchised is good for all children. All children benefit when the school environment is respectful and inclusive. All children benefit when inequitable knowledge frameworks and deficit thinking are replaced with more equitable facts and assumptions. The learning of all children is enhanced when school is about more than memorizing small chunks of information or passing tests. The learning of all children is enhanced when they can bring the totality of their lived experiences to the sense-making conversations of the classroom, without shame or blame, to be fully engaged in the learning activities at hand.

Burns called for a theory of leadership that is both transforming and empowering—one that permits people to "rise above narrow interests and work together for transcending goals" (2003, p. 26). In the quotation with which this book opened, he called for the quality of leadership to be assessed by "actual social change." This is the promise of transformative leadership and the reason why we, indeed, do need this additional theory of educational leadership.

Public education needs leadership—an army of educators who accept the mandate and take up the call. We do not need more technocrats or heroic or charismatic leaders. We do need committed and courageous educators who are determined to bring hope to the hopeless, inclusion to the marginalized, freedom to the oppressed, and to offer to every student the promise inherent in the constitution of the country in which they live—the promise of a "more perfect union." This must no longer be dependent on a child's zip code, on their parents' education or financial status, on the language they speak, or the religion they practice. It certainly must not be dependent on the school they happen to attend, the teacher to whom they happen to be assigned, or to the ideology and effectiveness of the school leader.

Transformation is possible. It is within our capabilities. It does not require new textbooks or new standards. It does not require additional resources or new facilities. But it does require, as Lisa Delpit would urge, that educators have "open hearts and minds," that we summon up our moral courage, speak up, and take action to create learning environments in which every child feels welcome and included. This is the role of the critical theory of transformative leadership, sought by Foster in the second quotation with which this book opened. It helps to provide more "adequate solutions" to the problems of inequity, marginalization, and injustice in our schools.

When children never have to consider whether they belong, they are free to concentrate on the learning experiences at hand. Burns (2003) claims that "the nub of leadership is a causal force—"the crucial link between intention and outcome" (p. 221). If the intent is to create schools that are inclusive, equitable, and socially just, then it is to that task we must turn our energies and commitment. With the dedication of transformative educational leaders, significant metamorphosis and transformation can occur. Although there are no maps, no blueprints, and no prescriptions, the framework of transformative leadership as described here can point the way.

In Burns's words:

> Leaders working as partners with the dispossessed people of the world to secure life, liberty, and the pursuit of happiness—happiness empowered with transforming purpose—could become the greatest act of united leadership the world has ever known. (2003, p. 3)

Let us join forces to make it happen!

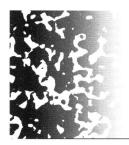

References

Cited in This Volume

Abbey-Lambertz, K. (2014, November 14). Detroit's staggering murder and violent crime rate are "a public health issue." *Huffington Post.* Retrieved July 2015 from http://www.huffingtonpost.com/2014/11/14/detroit-highest-murder-rate-violent-crime_n_6144460.html

Advancement Project. (2010). *Test, punish, and push out: How "zero-tolerance" and high stakes testing funnel youth into the school-to-prison pipeline.* Washington, DC: Author. Retrieved June 2015 from http://b.3cdn.net/advancement/d05cb2181a4545db07_r2im6caqe.pdf

Amnesty International. (2015). *The global refugee crisis: A conspiracy of neglect.* London: Author. Retrieved June 2015 from http://static.guim.co.uk/ni/1434356535972/The-Global-Refugee-Crisis-a.pdf

Anello, E., Hernandez, J., & Khadem, M. (2014). *Transformative leadership: Developing the hidden dimension.* [Kindle version]. Houston, TX: Harmony Equity.

Astin, A. W., & Astin, H. S. (2000). *Leadership reconsidered: Engaging higher education in social change.* Battle Creek, MI: Kellogg Foundation. Retrieved December 2006 from http://www.wkkf.org/knowledge-center/resources/2007/01/Leadership-Reconsidered-Engaging-Higher-Education-In-Social-Change.aspx

Austen, I. (2015, June 2). Canada's forced schooling of Aboriginal children was "cultural genocide," report finds. *New York Times*. Retrieved from http://www.nytimes.com/2015/06/03/world/americas/canadas-forced-schooling-of-aboriginal-children-was-cultural-genocide-report-finds.html

Bakhtin, M. M. (1973). *The problem of Dostoevsky's poetics*. Ann Arbor, MI: Ardis.

Bakhtin, M. M. (1981). *The dialogic imagination* (C. Emerson & M. Holquist, Trans.). Austin: University of Texas Press.

Bakhtin, M. M. (1984). *The problem of Dostoevsky's poetics*. Minneapolis: University of Minnesota Press.

Barber, B. R. (2001). An aristocracy of everyone. In S. J. Goodlad (Ed.), *The last best hope: A democracy reader* (pp. 2–22). San Francisco: Jossey-Bass.

Bennis, W., & Nanus, B. (1985). *Leaders: The strategies for taking charge*. New York: Harper & Row.

Bertrand, M., & Mullainathan, S. (2004). Are Emily and Greg more employable than Lakisha and Jamal? A field experiment on labor market discrimination. University of Chicago Graduate School of Business. Retrieved from http://web.mit.edu/cortiz/www/Diversity/Bertrand%20and%20Mullainathan,%202004.pdf

Bieneman, P. D. (2011). Transformative leadership: The exercise of agency in educational leadership. In C. M. Shields (Ed.), *Transformative leadership: A reader* (pp. 221–237). New York: Peter Lang.

Biesta, G. J. J., & Stams, G. J. J. M. (2001). Critical thinking and the question of critique: Some lessons from deconstruction. *Studies in Philosophy and Education, 20*, 57–74.

Blackmore, J. (2011). Leadership in pursuit of purpose: Social, economic, and political transformation. In C. M. Shields (Ed.), *Transformative leadership: A reader* (pp. 21–36). New York: Peter Lang.

Blake, R. R., & Mouton, J. S. (1964). *The managerial grid*. Houston, TX: Gulf.

BLS (Bureau of Labor Statistics). (2015). *Unemployment rates for the 50 largest cities*. Retrieved May 2015 from http://www.bls.gov/lau/lacilg10.htm

Bocian, D. G., Li, W., & Ernst, E. W. (2010, June 18). *Foreclosures by race and ethnicity: The demographics of a crisis*. Center for Responsible Lending. Retrieved from http://www.responsiblelending.org/mortgage-lending/research-analysis/foreclosures-by-race-and-ethnicity.pdf

Bode, B. H. (2001). Reorientation in education. In S. J. Goodlad (Ed.), *The last best hope: A democracy reader* (pp. 92–100). San Francisco: Jossey-Bass.

Bogotch, I., & Shields, C. M. (Eds.). (2013). *International handbook of educational leadership and social (in)justice*. Dordrecht: Springer.

Boske, C. (2012). *Educational leadership: Building bridges among ideas, schools, and nations*. Charlotte, NC: Information Age.

Bourdieu, P., with Passeron, J.-C. (1977). *Reproduction in education, society and culture*. London: Sage.

Brooks, J. S., & Tooms, A. K. (2008). A dialectic of social justice: Finding synergy between life and work through reflection and dialogue. *Journal of School Leadership, 18*(2), 134–163.

Brown, H. (2015, September 8). The role of racial tensions in state decisions to cut back welfare. Scholars Strategy Network. Retrieved September 2015 from http://thesocietypages.org/ssn/2015/09/08/race-and-welfare-cuts/

Buber, M. (1970). *I and thou* (W. Kaufman, Trans.). New York: Charles Scribner & Sons.

Burns, J. M. (1978). *Leadership.* New York: Harper & Row.

Burns, J. M. (2003). *Transforming leadership*. New York: Grove.

Byanyima, W. (2015). *Even it up.* Oxfam International. Retrieved September 2015 from https://www.oxfam.org/en/pressroom/pressreleases/2015-01-19/richest-1-will-own-more-all-rest-2016

Cáceres, M. (2014, June 18). Child migrants from Central America: "War refugees." *The World Post*. Retrieved June 2015 from http://www.huffingtonpost.com/marco-caceres/child-migrants-from-centr_b_5509861.html

Caldwell, C., Dixon, R. D., Floyd, L. A., Chaudoin, J., Post, J., & Cheokas, G. (2012). Transformative leadership: Achieving unparalleled excellence. *Journal of Business Ethics, 109*, 175–187.

Cambron-McCabe, N., & McCarthy, M. (2005). Educating school leaders for social justice. *Educational Policy, 19*(1), 201–222.

Capper, C. A. (1998). Critically oriented and postmodern perspectives: Sorting out the differences and applications for practice. *Educational Administration Quarterly, 34*(3), 354–379.

Chow, K. (2015). Grace Lee Boggs, activist and American revolutionary, turns 100. NPR. Retrieved June 27, 2015, from http://www.npr.org/sections/codeswitch/2015/06/27/417175523/grace-lee-boggs-activist-and-american-revolutionary-turns-100?utm_medium=RSS&utm_campaign=news

Ciulla, J. (2005). Ethics, chaos, and the demand for good leaders. In P. S. Temes (Ed.), *Teaching leadership* (pp. 181–201). New York: Peter Lang.

Coleman, M.-R., & Shah-Coltrane, S. (2015). Children of promise: Dr. James Gallagher's thoughts on underrepresentation within gifted education. *Journal for the Education of the Gifted, 38*(1), 70–76.

Coley, R. J., & Baker, B. (2013). *Poverty and education: Finding the way forward.* Princeton, NJ: Educational Testing Service. Retrieved June 2014 from http://www.ets.org/s/research/pdf/poverty_and_education_report.pdf

Collins, P. H. (1991). *Black feminist thought: Knowledge, consciousness, and the politics of empowerment.* New York: Routledge.

Covey, S. R. (1989). *The 7 habits of highly effective people* [Kindle version]. Retrieved from Amazon.com

CRDC (U.S. Department of Education Office for Civil Rights). (2014). Civil rights data collection: Data snapshot (School discipline). March 21, 2014. Retrieved July 2015 from http://ocrdata.ed.gov/Downloads/CRDC-School-Discipline-Snapshot.pdf

Davis, S. H. (2006). Influencing transformative learning for leaders. *School Administrator, 63*(8), 67–74.

Delpit, L. D. (1989). The silenced dialogue: Power and pedagogy in educating other people's children. In N. M. Hidalgo, C. L. McDowell, & E. V. Siddle (Eds.), *Facing racism in education.* Reprint Series No. 21 (1993). Cambridge, MA: Harvard Educational Review.

De Tocqueville, A. (1931). *Democracy in America.* Retrieved September 2015 from http://xroads.virginia.edu/~HYPER/DETOC/toc_intro.html

Detroit public school statistics. (2010). Real life. My music. Retrieved July 2015 from http://reallifemymusic.org/detroit-public-school-statistics/

Dewey, J. (1916/2008). *Democracy and education.* Project Gutenberg Ebook. Retrieved June 2015 from http://www.gutenberg.org/files/852/852-h/852-h.htm#link2H_SUMM

Dimmock, C., & Goh, J. W. P. (2011). Transformative pedagogy, leadership and school organisation for the twenty-first-century knowledge-based economy: The case of Singapore. *School Leadership & Management, 31*(3), 215–234.

DuFour, R., & DuFour, R. (2012). *The school leader's guide to professional learning communities at work.* Bloomington, IN: Solution Tree.

DuFour, R., Guidice, A., Magee, D., Martin, P., & Zivkovic, B. (2002). The student support team as a professional learning community. In C. D. Johnson & S. K. Johnson (Eds.), *Building stronger school counseling programs: Building futuristic approaches into the present.* ERIC, ED464270 & CG031690.

Eavis, P. (2014, April 12). Executive pay: Invasion of the supersalaries. *New York Times.* Retrieved September 2015 from http://www.nytimes.com/2014/04/13/business/executive-pay-invasion-of-the-supersalaries.html?_r=0

Ebrahim, Z. (2014). I am not my father. *Ted Talk.* Retrieved September 2015 from https://www.ted.com/talks/zak_ebrahim_i_am_

the_son_of_a_terrorist_here_s_how_i_chose_peace?language= en#t-530077

Eckholm, E. (2015, March 30). Religious protection laws, once called shields, are now seen as cudgels. *New York Times*. Retrieved from http://www.nytimes.com/2015/03/31/us/politics/religious-pro- tection-laws-once-called-shields-are-now-seen-as-cudgels.html

Ellsworth, E. (1989). Why doesn't this feel empowering? Working through the repressive myths of critical pedagogy. *Harvard Ed- ucational Review, 59*(3), 297–324.

Fine, S. (1997). Michigan and housing discrimination, 1949–1968. *Michigan Historical Review, 23*(2), 81–114.

Follett, M. P. (1918). *The new state: Group organization the solution of pop- ular government.* New York: Longmans, Green.

Follett, M. P. (1940/1973). *Dynamic administration: The collected pa- pers of Mary Parker Follett* (E. M. Fox & L. Urwick, Eds.). London: Pitman.

Ford, M., & Chandler, A. (2015, June 15). "Hate crime": A mass kill- ing at a historic church. *The Atlantic*. Retrieved from http://www. theatlantic.com/national/archive/2015/06/shooting-emanu- el-ame-charleston/396209/

Foster, W. (1982, March), *Toward a critical theory of educational admin- istration*, Paper presented at the annual meeting of the American Educational Research Association, New York.

Foster, W. (1983, April), *Leadership as praxis: Issues in administration*, Paper presented at the annual meeting of the American Educa- tional Research Association, Montreal.

Foster, W. (1986). *Paradigms and promises.* Buffalo, NY: Prometheus.

Freire, P. (1970). *Pedagogy of the oppressed* (M. B. Ramos, Trans.). New York: Herder & Herder.

Furman, G. C. (2004). The ethic of community. *Journal of Educational Administration, 42*(2), 215–235.

Giroux, H. A. (1993). Foreword. In W. G. Tierney (Ed.), *Communities of difference: Higher education in the twenty-first century.* Toronto: OISE.

Giroux, H. A. (2005). The terror of neoliberalism: Rethinking the sig- nificance of cultural politics. *College Literature, 32*(1), 1–19.

Giroux, H. A. (2009). Education and the crisis of youth: Schooling and the promise of democracy. *The Educational Forum, 73*, 8–18.

Green, J. M. (1999). *Deep democracy: Diversity, community, and transfor- mation.* Lanham, MD: Rowman & Littlefield.

Green Cup Challenge. (2015). Green Schools Alliance. Retrieved from http://www.greenschoolsalliance.org/program/green-cup- challenge.

Greene, M. (1973). *Teacher as stranger: Educational philosophy for the modern age*. Belmont, CA: Wadsworth.

Greene, M. (1998). Introduction: Teaching for social justice. In W. Ayers, J. A Hunt, & T. Quinn (Eds.), *Teaching for social justice* (pp. xxvii–xlvi). New York: Teachers College Press.

Greenleaf, R. K., & Spears, L. C. (1998). *The power of servant leadership*. San Francisco: Berrett-Koehler.

Grumet, M. R. (1995). The curriculum: What are the basics and are we teaching them? In J. L. Kincheloe & S. R. Steinberg (Eds.), *Thirteen questions* (2nd ed., pp. 15–21). New York: Peter Lang.

Gurevich, M. (1961). *The social structure of acquaintanceship networks*. Cambridge, MA: MIT Press.

Hallinger, P., Leithwood, K., & Heck, R. H. (2010). Leadership: Instructional. In E. Baker, P. Peterson, & B. McGaw (Eds.), *International encyclopedia of education* (3rd ed., pp. 18–25). Oxford: Elsevier.

Hallinger, P., & Murphy, J. (1985). Assessing the instructional management behavior of principals. *Elementary School Journal, 86*(2), 217–247.

Headlee, C. (2007). Detroit has worst high-school graduation rate. NPR [Radio interview]. Retrieved July 2015 from http://www.npr.org/templates/story/story.php?storyId=11601692

Hersey, P., & Blanchard, K. H. (1977). *Management of organizational behavior* (3rd ed.). Englewood Cliffs, NJ: Prentice-Hall.

Hitchens, C. (2008, May). How to be a public intellectual. *Prospect Magazine, 146*.

ICPH (Institute for Children, Poverty, and Homelessness). (2013). Improving special education services for homeless students with disabilities. *America Almanac*. Retrieved May 30, 2014, from http://www.icphusa.org/PDF/americanalmanac/Almanac_Issue_Special%20Ed.pdf

Jensen, E. (2013). *Engaging students with poverty in mind: Practical strategies for raising achievement*. [Kindle version]. Alexandria, VA: ASCD.

Kenway, J., & Modra, H. (1992). Feminist pedagogy and emancipatory possibilities. In C. Luke & J. Gore (Eds.), *Feminisms and critical pedagogy* (pp. 138–166). New York: Routledge.

KIDS COUNT data book. (2015). Annie E. Casey Foundation. Retrieved June 2015 from http://www.aecf.org/m/resourcedoc/aecf-2015kidscountdatabook-2015.pdf

Kilkenny, A. (2009). Philadelphia private swim club forces out black children. *Huffington Post*. Retrieved June 2015 from http://www.huffingtonpost.com/allison-kilkenny/philadelphia-private-swim_b_228253.html

King, T. (2015, June 11). No justice for Canada's First Peoples. *New York Times.* Retrieved June 2015 from http://www.nytimes.com/2015/06/12/opinion/thomas-king-no-justice-for-canadas-first-peoples.html?_r=0

Kosciw, J. G., Greytak, E. A., Palmer, N. A., & Boesen, M. J. (2014). *The 2013 national school climate survey: The experiences of lesbian, gay, bisexual, and transgender youth in our nation's schools.* New York: GLSEN.

Kowalski, J., & Oates, A. (1993). The evolving role of superintendents in school-based management. *Journal of School Leadership, 3,* 380–390.

Kristof, N. (2013, November 6). Slavery isn't a thing of the past. *New York Times.* Retrieved from http://www.nytimes.com/2013/11/07/opinion/slavery-isnt-a-thing-of-the-past.html?_r=0

Labaree, D. F. (1997). Public goods, private goods: The American struggle over educational goals. *American Educational Research Journal, 34*(1), 39–81.

Ladson-Billings, G. (2015). Social justice in education award lecture. AERA. Retrieved July 2015 from http://www.aera.net/Events-Meetings/AnnualMeeting/PreviousAnnualMeetings/2015AnnualMeeting/2015AnnualMeetingWebcasts/SocialJusticeinEducationAward(2015)LectureGloriaJLadson-Billings/tabid/15943/Default.aspx

Langlois, L. (2011). *The anatomy of ethical leadership.* Edmonton, Canada: Athabaska.

Lauder, H. (1991). Education, democracy, and the economy. *British Journal of Education, 12,* 417–431. Reprinted in A. H. Halsey, H. Lauder, P. Brown, & A. S. Wells (Eds.). (2003). *Education: Culture, economy, society* (pp. 382–392). Oxford: Oxford University Press.

Leithwood, K. (2010). Transformational school leadership. In E. Baker, B. McGaw, & P. Peterson (Eds.), *International encyclopedia of education* (3rd ed.). Oxford: Elsevier.

Leithwood, K., & Chapman, J. D. (1999). *International handbook of educational leadership and administration.* Norwell, MA: Kluwer.

Leithwood, K., & Chapman, J. D. (2002). *Second international handbook of educational leadership and administration.* Dordrecht & Boston: Kluwer Academic.

Leithwood, K., & Duke, D. (1998). A century's quest to understand school leadership. In J. Murphy & K. S. Lewis (Eds.), *Handbook of research on educational administration* (pp. 45–72). San Francisco: Jossey-Bass.

Leithwood, K., & Jantzi, D. (1999). Transformational school leadership effects: A replication. *School Effectiveness and School Improvement, 10*(4), 451–479.

Lindholm-Leary, K. J. (2001). *Dual language education.* Clevedon, UK: Multilingual Matters.

Lynn, M., & Parker, L. (2006). Critical race studies in education: Examining a decade of research on U.S. Schools. *The Urban Review, 38*(4), 257–290.

Macedo, D. (1995). Power and education: Who decides the forms schools have taken, and who should decide? In J. L. Kincheloe & S. R. Steinberg, *Thirteen questions* (pp. 43–57). New York: Peter Lang.

Mahbubani, K. (2013, August 20). The new global ethic. *The World Post*. Retrieved July 2015 from http://www.huffingtonpost.com/kishore-mahbubani/the-new-global-ethic_b_3467882.html

Marks, H. M., & Printy, S. M. (2003). Principal leadership and school performance: An integration of transformational and instructional leadership. *Educational Administration Quarterly, 39*(3), 370–397.

Markus, B. P. (2015, June 27). Who's burning black churches? Arsonists hit at least 3 southern congregations in the last 7 days. *RawStory*. Retrieved June 2015 from http://www.rawstory.com/2015/06/whos-burning-black-churches-arsonists-hit-at-least-3-southern-congregations-in-the-last-7-days/

Martens, J. (2015). *9 step leadership program.* Amazon digital services.

Martin, P. (2013). Human trafficking: Modern-day "slavery" in America. WGBH News. Retrieved June 2015 from http://wgbhnews.org/post/human-trafficking-modern-day-slavery-america

Maxwell, J. C. (2013). *The 5 levels of leadership: Proven steps to maximize your potential.* New York: Hachette/Center Street.

Maxwell, J. C., & Ziglar, Z. (2007). *21 irrefutable laws of leadership.* Nashville, TN: Nelson.

McKenzie, K. B., Cambron-McCabe, N., Capper, C. A., Christman, D. E., Dantey, M., Gonzalez, M. L., Hernandez, F., Fierro, E., & Scheurich, J. J. (2008). From the field: A proposal for educating leaders for social justice. *Educational Administration Quarterly, 44*(1), 111–138.

Melzer, A. M. (2003). What is an intellectual? In A. M. Melzer, J. Weinberger, & M. R. Zinman (Eds.), *The public intellectual* (pp. 3–14). Lanham, MD: Rowman & Littlefield.

Melzer, A. M., Weinberger, J., & Zinman, M. R. (Eds.). (2003). *The public intellectual.* New York: Rowman & Littlefield.

Merz, C., & Furman, G. C. (1997). *Community and schools: Promise and paradox.* New York: Teachers College Press.

Mezirow, J. (1991). *Transformative dimensions of adult learning.* San Francisco: Jossey-Bass.

Mezirow, J. (1996). Contemporary paradigms of learning. *Adult Education Quarterly, 46*(3), 158–172.

Miller, P., Brown, T., & Hopson, R. (2011). Centering love, hope, and trust in the community: Transformative urban leadership informed by Paulo Freire. *Urban Education, 46*(5), 1078–1099.

Mohan, E. (2009). *A call for engagement: Educational leaders as activists and public intellectuals.* Paper presented at the annual meeting of the American Education Research Association Conference, San Diego, CA.

Mohan, E. (2011). From cowardice to courage: Breaking the silence surrounding race in schools. In C. M. Shields (Ed.), *Transformative leadership: A* reader (pp. 53–62). New York: Peter Lang.

Møller, J. (2010). Leadership: Democratic. In E. Baker, P. Peterson, & B. McGaw (Eds.), *International encyclopedia of education* (3rd ed., pp. 12–17). Oxford: Elsevier.

Moore, K. A., Redd, Z., Burkhauser, M., Mbwana, M. A. K., & Collins, A. (2009). *Children in poverty: Trends, consequences, and policy options.* Child Trends Research Brief. Retrieved July 2015 from http://www.childtrends.org/wp-content/uploads/2013/11/2009-11Children-inPoverty.pdf

Mudallali, A. (2013). *The Syrian refugee crisis is pushing Lebanon to the brink.* Woodrow Wilson International Center for Scholars. Retrieved June 2015 from http://www.wilsoncenter.org/sites/default/files/syrian_refugee_crisis_pushing_lebanon_to_brink.pdf

NAACP (National Association for the Advancement of Colored People). (2015). Criminal Justice Fact Sheet. Retrieved September 2015 from http://www.naacp.org/pages/criminal-justice-fact-sheet

Naisbitt, J., & Naisbitt, N. (2001). *High tech, high touch: Technology and our search for meaning.* London: Nicholas Brealey.

Naples, N. A., & Fraser, N. (2004). To interpret the world and to change it: An interview with Nancy Fraser. *Signs: Journal of Women and Culture in Society, 29*(4), 1103–1123.

National Center on Inclusive Education, (n.d.), Who cares about Kelsey? Retrieved November 2015 from http://www.whocaresaboutkelsey.com/docs/educational-materials/key-statistics.pdf?sfvrsn=2

NCES (National Center for Educational Statistics). (2010). Status and trends in the education of racial and ethnic minorities. Retrieved June 2015 from https://nces.ed.gov/pubs2010/2010015/indicator7_28.asp

Nearly half of Detroit's adults are functionally illiterate, report finds. (2011, May 7). *Huff Post.* Retrieved September 2015 from http://www.huffingtonpost.com/2011/05/07/detroit-illiteracy-nearly-half-education_n_858307.html

Nussbaum, M. C. (2006). *Frontiers of justice* [Kindle version]. Retrieved from Amazon.com

Oakes, J., & Rogers, J. (2006). *Learning power: Organizing for education and justice.* New York: Teachers College Press.

Obama, B. H. (2015, June 26). Transcript: Obama's remarks on Supreme Court ruling on same-sex marriage. *The Washington Post.* Retrieved June 2015 from http://www.washingtonpost.com/news/post-nation/wp/2015/06/26/transcript-obamas-remarks-on-supreme-court-ruling-on-same-sex-marriage/

OCR (U.S. Department of Education Office of Civil Rights). (2012). *Revealing new truths about our nation's schools.* Retrieved from http://www2.ed.gov/about/offices/list/ocr/docs/crdc-2012-data-summary.pdf

Ogawa, R. T., & Bossert, S. T. (1995). Leadership as an organizational quality. *Educational Administration Quarterly, 31*(2), 224–243.

Palmer, P. J. (1998). *The courage to teach.* San Francisco: Jossey-Bass.

Peterson, M. D. (1984). *Thomas Jefferson: Writings.* New York: Library of America.

Pfaff, W. (2010). *The irony of Manifest Destiny: The tragedy of America's foreign policy.* New York: Walker & Co.

Pinar, W. F. (2011). *What is curriculum theory?* New York: Routledge.

Puritan life. (n.d.). U.S. History. Retrieved August 2015 from http://www.ushistory.org/us/3d.asp

Rosich, K. J. (2007). *Race, ethnicity, and the criminal justice system.* Washington, DC: American Sociological Association. Available at http://asanet.org

Said, E. W. (1994). Representations of the intellectual. In E. W. Said (Ed.), *Representations of the intellectual: The 1993 Reith lectures* (pp. 3–17). London: Random House.

Scheurich, J. J., & Young, M. D. (1997). Coloring epistemologies: Are our research epistemologies racially biased? *Educational Researcher, 4*(26), 4–16.

Schwartz, P., & Ogilvy, J. (1979). *The emergent paradigm: Changing patterns of thought and belief.* Ann Arbor, MI: SRI International.

Sears, J. (1993). Responding to the sexual diversity of faculty and students: Sexual praxis and the critically reflective administrator. In C. A. Capper (Ed.), *Educational administration in a pluralistic society* (pp. 110–172). Albany: State University of New York Press.

Sen, A. (1992). *Inequality reexamined* [Kindle edition]. Retrieved from Amazon.com

Sergiovanni, T. J. (1994). Organizations or communities? Changing the metaphor changes the theory. *Educational Administration Quarterly, 30*(2), 214–226.

Shields, C. M., (2008), *Courageous leadership for transforming schools: Democratizing practice*, Lanham, MD: Rowman & Littlefield.

Shields, C. M. (2010). Transformative leadership: Working for equity in diverse contexts. *Educational Administration Quarterly, 46*(4), 558–589.

Shields, C. M. (2011). Transformative leadership: An introduction. In C. M. Shields (Ed.), *Transformative leadership: A reader* (pp. 1–17). New York: Peter Lang.

Shields, C. M. (2013). *Transformative leadership in education: Equitable change in an uncertain and complex world.* New York: Routledge.

Shields, C. M. (2013). Leadership for social justice education: A critical transformative approach. In I. Bogotch & C. M. Shields (2013), *International handbook of educational leadership and social (in)justice* (pp. 323–340.). Dordrecht: Springer.

Shields, C. M., Bishop, R., & Mazawi, A. E. (2005). *Pathologizing practices: The impact of deficit thinking on education.* New York: Peter Lang.

Shields, C. M., & Edwards, M. M. (2005). *Dialogue is not just talk: A new ground for educational leadership.* New York: Peter Lang.

Sidorkin, A, M. (1999). *Beyond discourse: Education, the self, and dialogue.* Albany: State University of New York Press.

Sidorkin, A. M. (2002). *Learning relations: Impure education, deschooled schools, and dialogue with evil.* New York: Peter Lang.

Skiba, R. J., & Rausch, M. K. (2006). Zero tolerance, suspension, and expulsion: Questions of equity and effectiveness. In C. M. Evertson & C. S. Weinstein (Eds.), *Handbook of classroom management: Research, practice, and contemporary issues* (pp. 1063–1089). Mahwah, NJ: Lawrence Erlbaum.

Stanford Encyclopedia of philosophy. (2005). Stanford, CA: Stanford Center for the Study of Language.

Starratt, R. J. (1991). Building an ethical school: A theory for practice in educational leadership. *Educational Administration Quarterly, 27*(2), 185–202.

Starratt, R. J. (2005). The spirituality of presence for educational leaders. In C. M. Shields, M. M. Edwards, & A. Sayani (Eds.), *Inspiring practice: Spirituality and educational leadership* (pp. 67–84). Lancaster, PA: ProActive.

State high school graduation rates by race, ethnicity. (2015). Governing.com. Retrieved June 2015 from http://www.governing.com/gov-data/education-data/state-high-school-graduation-rates-by-race-ethnicity.html

Stiglitz, J. E. (2011). Of the 1%, by the 1%, for the 1%. *Vanity Fair.* Retrieved March 2015 from http://www.vanityfair.com/news/2011/05/top-one-percent-201105

Stillwell, R., & Sable, J. (2013). Public school graduates and dropouts from the common core of data: School year 2009–10. NCES.

Retrieved June 2015 from http://nces.ed.gov/pubs2013/2013309. pdf

Stone, A. (2014). *Leadership: 7 simple leadership secrets that will make you a great leader people will follow* [Kindle version]. Retrieved from Amazon.com

Sun Tzu. (545BCE/1972). *The art of war.* Retrieved September 2015 from http://www.sonshi.com/original-the-art-of-war-translation-notgiles.html

Swartz, D. (1997). *Culture and power: The sociology of Pierre Bourdieu.* Chicago: Chicago University Press.

Sweeten, G. (2006). Who will graduate? Disruption of high school education by arrest and court involvement. *Justice Quarterly, 23*(4), 462–480.

Taylor, E. W. (2006). The challenge of teaching for change. *New Directions for Adult and Continuing Education, 112,* 91–95.

Terry, R. W. (1993). *Authentic leadership: Courage in action.* San Francisco: Jossey-Bass.

Texas Ordinance of Secession. (1861, February 21). Retrieved from http://www.lsjunction.com/docs/secession.htm

Thayer-Bacon, B. J. (2001). Radical democratic communities always-in-the-making. *Studies in Philosophy and Education, 20*(1), 5–25.

Theoharis, G. (2007). Social justice educational leaders and resistance: Toward a theory of social justice leadership. *Educational Administration Quarterly, 43*(2), 221–258.

Tierney, W. G. (1993). *Communities of difference: Higher education in the twenty-first century.* Toronto: OISE.

Tomlinson, S. (2013, January 31). Revealed: How immigrants in America are sending $120 BILLION to their struggling families back home. *The Daily Mail.* Retrieved June 2015 from http://www.dailymail.co.uk/news/article-2271455/Revealed-How-immigrants-America-sending-120-BILLION-struggling-families-home.html

Tooms, A.K., & Boske, C. (2010). *Bridge leadership.* Charlotte, NC: Information Age.

Torres, C. A. (1998). *Democracy, education, and multiculturalism.* New York: Rowman & Littlefield.

Trujillo, T., & Renée, M. (2013, Winter–Spring). Democratic school turnarounds: Pursuing equity and learning from evidence. *Voices in Urban Education, 36,* 18–26.

Truong, K. (2015, July 9). How Jenny Horne's plea helped bring down Confederate flag in South Carolina. *The Christian Science Monitor.* Retrieved July 2015 from http://www.csmonitor.com/USA/USA-Update/2015/0709/How-Jenny-Horne-s-plea-helped-bring-down-Confederate-flag-in-South-Carolina-video

UNESCO (United Nations Educational, Scientific and Cultural Organization). (2010). *Education counts: Towards the millennium developed goals.* Retrieved from http://unesdoc.unesco.org/images/0019/001902/190214e.pdf

USDE (U.S. Department of Education). (2010). *College- and career-ready standards and assessments.* Retrieved August 2015 from https://www2.ed.gov/policy/elsec/leg/blueprint/faq/college-career.pdf

USDE (U.S. Department of Education). (2014). *Expansive survey of America's public schools reveals troubling racial disparities.* Retrieved June 2014 from http://www.ed.gov/news/press-releases/expansive-survey-americas-public-schools-reveals-troubling-racial-disparities

Valencia, R. R. (Ed.). (1997). *The evolution of deficit thinking.* London: Falmer.

Valencia, R. R. (2010). *Dismantling contemporary deficit thinking: Educational thought and practice.* New York: Routledge.

Wagstaff, L., & Fusarelli, L. (1995). Establishing collaborative governance and leadership. In P. Reyes, J. Scribner, & A. Scribner (Eds.), *Lessons from high-performing Hispanic schools: Creating learning communities* (pp. 19–35). New York: Teachers College Press.

Warren, M. R., Thompson, J. P., & Saegert, S. (2001). The role of social capital in combating poverty. In S. Saegert, J. P. Thompson, & M. R. Warren (Eds.), *Social capital and poor communities* (pp. 1–28). New York: Russell Sage Foundation.

Wearmount, J., & Berryman, M. (2012). Viewing restorative approaches to addressing challenging behavior of minority ethnic students through a community of practice lens. *Cambridge Journal of Education, 42*(2), 253–268.

Weick, K. E. (1996). Fighting fires in educational administration. *Educational Administration Quarterly, 32*(4), 565–578.

Weiner, E. J. (2003). Secretary Paulo Freire and the democratization of power: Toward a theory of transformative leadership. *Educational Philosophy and Theory, 35*(1), 89–106.

Westheimer, J., & Kahn, J. (2004). What kind of citizen? The politics of educating for democracy. *American Educational Research Journal, 41*(2), 237–269.

Wrigley, T. (2013). Rethinking school effectiveness and improvement: A question of paradigms. *Discourse: Studies in the Cultural Politics of Education, 34*(1), 31–47.

Wynne, J. T. (2015). Living with the dark and the dazzling: Unlearning racism. In L. D. Drakeford (Ed.), *The race controversy in American education, Vol. 2* (pp. 363–385). Santa Barbara, CA: Praeger.

Yettick, H., & Lloyd, S. C. (2015, May 29). Graduation rate hits high, but some groups lag. *Education Week.* Retrieved August 2015 from

http://www.edweek.org/ew/articles/2015/06/04/graduation-rate-hits-high-but-some-groups.html

Yukl, G. (1994). *Leadership in organizations* (3rd ed.). Englewood Cliffs, NJ: Prentice-Hall.

Other Resources for Transformative Leadership

Dantley. M. (2003). Critical spirituality: Enhancing transformative leadership through critical theory and African American prophetic spirituality. *International Journal of Leadership in Education, 18*(4), 3–17.

Duncan, M., Alperstein, M., Mayers, P., Olckers, L., & Gibbs, T. (2006). Not just another multi-professional course! Part 1. Rationale for a transformative curriculum. *Medical Teacher, 28*(1), 59–63.

Keddie, A. (2006). Pedagogies and critical reflection: Key understandings for transformative gender justice. *Gender and Education, 18*(1), 99–114.

Miettinen, R. (2006). Epistemology of transformative material activity: John Dewey's pragmatism and cultural-historical activity theory. *Journal for the Theory of Social Behaviour, 36*(4), 390–408.

Quantz, R. A., Rogers, J., & Dantley, M. (1991). Rethinking transformative leadership: Toward democratic reform of schools. *Journal of Education, 173*(3), 96–118.

Shields, C. M. (2003). Dialogic leadership for social justice: Overcoming pathologies of silence. *Educational Administrative Quarterly, 11*(1), 111–134.

Shields, C. M. (2003). *Good intentions are not enough. Transformative leadership for communities of difference.* Lanham, MD: Scarecrow.

Transformative Leadership in Education. Website and blog companions to C. M. Shields, *Transformative leadership in education.* Accessible at http://routledgetextbooks.com/textbooks/_author/shields-9780415892544/default.php

Transformative Leadership. (2015). YouTube video produced by Shields, C. M., and T. Zook, Producers). Available at https://www.youtube.com/watch?v=7YEsZNbfg-c

Index

Peter Lang
PRIMERS
in Education

Peter Lang Primers are designed to provide a brief and concise introduction or supplement to specific topics in education. Although sophisticated in content, these primers are written in an accessible style, making them perfect for undergraduate and graduate classroom use. Each volume includes a glossary of key terms and a References and Resources section.

Other published and forthcoming volumes cover such topics as:

- Standards
- Popular Culture
- Critical Pedagogy
- Literacy
- Higher Education
- John Dewey
- Feminist Theory and Education
- Studying Urban Youth Culture
- Multiculturalism through Postformalism
- Creative Problem Solving
- Teaching the Holocaust
- Piaget and Education
- Deleuze and Education
- Foucault and Education

Look for more Peter Lang Primers to be published soon. To order other volumes, please contact our Customer Service Department:

      800-770-LANG (within the US)
      212-647-7706 (outside the US)
      212-647-7707 (fax)

To find out more about this and other Peter Lang book series, or to browse a full list of education titles, please visit our website:

    www.peterlang.com